The Roses at the End of the Road

Pat Leuchtman

Drawings by Henry Leuchtman

Fiftyshift.com Publishing

ISBN 9780984200016

Published by
Fiftyshift.com Publishing

Book Design by ReilleyDesign.com

CommonWeeder.com

For Henry
who makes all things possible.

Contents

My Life Before Roses

Did I ever dream I would be known as The Rose Lady? Absolutely not.

I never gave roses a second thought. My grandmother had a rose bush of some sort, and my father, like every other homeowner in our suburb, had a pink rambler on a split rail fence. I received my share of sweetheart rose corsages during high school. The roses were sweet, and I was pleased, but I never thought about their days in the garden.

After I married I did not yearn for a garden, but a yard came with our first house, a big old Victorian in Connecticut. We moved in March, a good time to think about a garden, but a month later my fourth child, Betsy, was born. Philip, the oldest, was only four and a half. No time to think about gardens. It took another year before I was ready to plant a hedge of lilacs along the back property line and marigolds by the kitchen door.

The lilacs were soon joined by a stockade fence to keep out our neighbor's energetic dogs, not a good mix for my children, who now numbered five.

The marigolds did fine, baking as they did in the hot sun that bounced off the bit of patio outside the kitchen door. That patio was useless for sitting and relaxing because there was no scrap of shade. All the shade was in front of the house where ancient maples lined our appropriately named Maple Street.

I loved living in that house with small children. My next door neighbor had seven children including two sets of twins. She was slightly older and very wise and loving. After the death of her grandmother who lived with them, she allowed Number Two Son Chris, who was about five, to go with them when they visited the nearby cemetery to tend the grandmother's grave. Chris said the cemetery was a good place to think. I began to realize that I could also look to my children for wisdom.

In that house I learned to bake bread. I was a Cub Scout Den leader and baked thousands of cookies. I read to the children after their baths every night and imagined myself a modern Mary Poppins. You will recall that Mary Poppins never had a garden.

Our second house was on a busy street, in a busy town, but the children were able to use a dirt service road behind the house. This road went through a woodland used by all the neighborhood children as they ran from house to house and friend to friend. All traffic in and out of the house was through the back door. Once a policeman showed up at that back door with 10-year-old Philip who had been caught setting off Halloween firecrackers. When I asked Philip what he thought he was doing he shrugged, and said "The policeman yelled stop – but I was the only one of my friends who stopped." That wasn't actually the question I was asking.

The extent of my gardening in this house was limited to battling bindweed that grew all around the foundation, and painting a cabinet for the patio a lovely shade of yellow called Primrose. It would be a long time before I would actually be able to recognize a primrose. That cabinet, collected from a curbside during a municipal 'get rid of everything' trash pick up, didn't house garden tools because there was no garden, only lawn and trees, and bindweed. The cabinet was just part of my fantasy of having lovely garden parties on the shady patio. Soon those particular fantasies came to an end.

Life on a suburban road also ended in 1971 when I divorced. I had not yet found my passion, but I was about to step onto the road that would end in a rose garden.

After the divorce I picked up my five children, Philip 12, Chris, 11, Diane 10, Betsy 8 and Kate 6, and abandoned the expensive Connecticut suburb where we had been living.

Through my friendship with suburban neighbors who owned a share in a farmhouse in western Massachusetts I became familiar with the area and decided that Greenfield was the place for us. Greenfield is a small town where living would be less expensive. I bought another big old Victorian house near the center of town and opened a craft gallery and shop named The Adventure.

Did I have business experience? No.

Did I know what I was doing? No.

However, my ignorance gave me confidence and I was sure that whatever happened, it would be an adventure. That much proved to be true.

As I settled into my new neighborhood and new business I gradually met Terry and Elliot who made leather belts and bags and sold wooden bowls and hippie dresses in the shop across the street. Their friend Henry sometimes worked for them.

One day a long Indian print dress appeared in the window. I really liked the sunny print and went in to try it on. It felt a little tight across the shoulders. Although I have always been proud of my 'swimmer's shoulders' they are sometimes a problem for me. I asked Henry if the dress looked too tight. He said no, it looked great. Pleased with his review I laid down my fifteen dollars and walked out with the dress.

Alas, it did not take long for it to split at the shoulders. "I knew it would," Henry confessed later, "but what could I say? That dress was the biggest sale my friends had all week."

I was to learn the financial realties of shopkeeping myself pretty quick. By the time I put the shop to bed eighteen months later, I had a steady job as a school reading aide and Henry had moved in with me and the children. That was the beginning of our adventures together.

With the shop closed, and a regular paycheck in my pocket, I finally did the sensible thing. I went back to school and finished my degree at the University of Massachusetts in Amherst. During that time, Henry and I would often sit in the Turkish Corner, a daybed wrapped in hippie bedspreads and tucked into a bay window, where we dreamed of life in the country.

One day, while sitting together in the Turkish Corner, Henry was reading me the comics and burst out laughing. One of his favorite characters, Beetle Bailey, had asked the Sarge where he was born. Pork Corners was the answer. "Outtasight! Outtasight!" responded Beetle Bailey enthusiastically in comic book fashion using one of Henry's favorite phrases. From that time on we referred to our mythical Shangri La as Pork Corners.

We would have vegetable gardens, berries and chickens. Maybe even pigs. I never thought about roses, or any flower except marigolds that might keep harmful nematodes at bay.

In preparation for Pork Corners we studied Organic Gardening Magazine and planted our tiny side yard with vegetables. Organic, of course. I was thrilled when a dinner guest sent a thank you gift of a load of horse manure. We bought a beehive and joined the local beekeepers association.

After my UMass graduation we bid Greenfield farewell, and set off for Maine where I had accepted a teaching job. Just what we wanted.

We named our new house Ant and Bee Farm. First, because

I loved Angela Banner's delightful little *Ant and Bee* books for children, discovered during my UMass education classes. Second, because we brought our beehive with us, and third, because our sandy Maine soil did indeed have lots of ants.

I began my teaching career. Over the year I learned a lot about the group psychology of sixth graders - and about myself. The teaching became more and more difficult for me. I wished I had the authority of the third grade teacher, Mrs. Fletcher, whose management skills remained fresh in my students' minds. In addition to teaching she worked on a lobster boat and took a no-nonsense view of life. The boys in my class remembered that if you got too rambunctious Mrs. Fletcher would pick you up by your belt and hang you on one of the coat hooks that lined the wall. They still shuddered at the memory.

My children made friends with the neighbor kids and learned the best places to drink beer and smoke and how to burn holes in each other's winter coats.

My teaching schedule and angst were not our whole life. We became members of the Maine Organic Farmers and Gardeners and planted a garden that was much too big for a first effort. Our elderly neighbor, Mr. Leslie, was an experienced gardener but he was always ready to lean on his hoe from time to time and "swap a few lies."

We bought chicks and two piglets, naming them Lunch and Dinner. We didn't want the children to be under any illusions. We kept our spirits up.

In June I retired from teaching forever. Henry suggested that since his brother wanted to leave New York, we all move to the ancestral apartment in Manhattan where he had grown up.

New York certainly wasn't Pork Corners, but it would be another adventure.

Before we could move we had to deal with the beehive, the chicks and the piglets. Fortunately, a new Maine friend took the beehive, and we persuaded my aunt and uncle to take the other animals. It is one thing to pack young chickens in crates and move them, but quite another to push two curious hundred-pound pigs into a VW bus for the drive to their new home. I always wondered what other drivers on the road that day thought as they passed two pink snouts and four beady eyes peering at them through the bus window.

Our move was timed so that I could wake up in the city of my birth on my thirty-fifth birthday. We stored furniture in my parent's barn, shipped lots of stuff to the city by UPS, and carried the rest in suitcases, backpacks and wicker baskets on the train. The children were disgruntled, appalled that we looked like immigrants – but it wasn't the first time members of our family were immigrants in New York.

It was so hot when we woke up on August 2, 1975 that official permission was given to open the fire hydrants for children to play in. The children became less gruntled as they enjoyed this New York tradition.

The ancestral apartment did have a small shady backyard. We never improved on the modest plantings there because I was only interested in growing vegetables and Henry feared that the soil was contaminated with heavy metals. He said he refused to eat anything grown in that soil. Our fantasies did not die, but they were packed away for a while.

I still had no interest in roses – except for the supermarket roses I put in my bridal bouquet. Henry and I had decided to make it legal.

Essentially we eloped, telling no one but the children. Philip, my oldest, was 18 and could act as Best Man and official witness. Chris, Diane, Betsy, and Kate, the youngest at 13, made up the rest of our wedding party. We wanted a real New York wedding and chose the Municipal Building downtown for our ceremony. Nothing could be more New York.

August 12 was possibly the hottest and most humid day of that year, but at the appointed hour we set off for the subway, we ladies carrying our homemade bouquets of supermarket roses. Some wedding parties like limousines or horse-drawn carriages, but we thought the subway was the only appropriate transportation for a New York wedding. We startled mid-day riders, one of whom leaped up to give me his seat, but we smiled at everyone and occasionally Henry bent down to laugh and give me a kiss.

We debarked at the Municipal Building and processed into the wedding waiting-room filled with a large East Indian family, gorgeous in gold and red saris and jangling gold bangles, with lively tots racing up and down the aisle. There were other less exotic couples like the sophisticated bride and groom sitting in front of us practicing being married. She'd whisper, "Ohhhh, I don't know. I'll have to ask my husband what he thinks." He'd clear his throat with a gruff, "Oh, I'll have to ask the old ball and chain," and then they'd laugh together at the absurdity of it all.

Finally our names were called and we gathered up our bouquets and marched to the front desk expecting to pass into the 'wedding room.' But no, we were stopped to sign an enormous ledger covered in scarlet buckram. We were amazed. We felt we might as well have been in a medieval chapel.

In fact, when next we were called we did go through the frosted office door, leaving the glare of the sweltering waiting-room, entering into a dim and frigid chapel-like room that even had a stained glass window. The clerk stood behind a lectern in lieu of a small pulpit. The shock of the air conditioning and the chapel atmosphere was so great that we remember very little of the ceremony which means that whenever either one of us needs something to be done, and the other is reluctant, the final word is, "You promised at our wedding -- to lay a terrace, go to the opera, take down the screens, clean out the closet," or whatever task is at issue. There is no denying we might have promised that very thing. Neither of us can remember the promises.

During our honeymoon sea voyage on the Staten Island Ferry with the kids one of the boatmen shook his head and muttered, "There's another one. Into the drink."

Back at the ancestral apartment on 19th Street we prepared

to greet friends who never suspected that our insistent dinner invitation was really an invitation to our very informal wedding reception. Pizza and Italian wedding cake from Veniero's, the famous Italian bakery nearby.

Actually, after we were hitched I telephoned my brother and his wife who worked at a law firm on Wall Street. Neither one of them was available, so I left a simple message. "Please tell him Mrs. Leuchtman called."

They got the hint and brought champagne.

The End Is In Sight

The tale of four years in the little apartment in the big city with five teenagers is too packed with incident to tell here. By the time we decided we had to leave the city, Philip and Chris had both graduated from high school, Philip to a job and an apartment of his own, and Chris to college. The three girls would come with us.

We thought about returning to Maine and our rural fantasy, Pork Corners, but Maine seemed so far away – and land was not cheap if you wanted to be near the water. Maybe Pork Corners was back in western Massachusetts where Henry had bought thirty seven acres in Heath years before and where we still had friends.

However, there was no house on his property so I left Henry with the children and went on a preliminary scouting mission. I drove around with the realtor but somehow the properties we saw were either too expensive or held no appeal. Near the end of one afternoon the realtor sighed and said she could show me one other property, but the financing might be complicated. I always ignore words like complicated so we set off for Heath, turning off

Route 8A and onto a dirt road that rambled through the woods before turning off onto another dirt road through open fields.

We drove up a slight hill and curved around in front of a tumble down red farmhouse with a porch that was slowly but surely sinking into the ground. We entered through the woodshed, complete with a two-holer against the back wall, and then into what the realtor called a summer kitchen with equipment from the 1930's. The downstairs bedroom and living space were bright with autumnal sunlight, and the big stone fireplace promised cozy winter evenings. There were three bedrooms and a second bath upstairs. Plenty of room for the five of us.

After we toured the house the realtor and I sat at the edge of the weedy lawn in the shade of an ancient apple tree. We nibbled on a couple of the windfalls while I looked at the house with its collapsing porch and a huge rugosa bush out front, still putting out a few pink roses. I wondered if the owners had brought a root back from a seaside vacation and planted it as a happy memento.

I was not oblivious to the flaws of the property, the lack of a 'real' kitchen, wavy floors, dark barnboarded walls, and that sinking porch that said nothing good about foundations, yet as I sat under that dazzling September sky and looked at the fields surrounded by woods, and circled by gentle hills just beginning to flame I wondered whether we would ever be able to buy such a beautiful spot.

However, the owner had been using the house as a summer home and his life was changing. In his eagerness to sell as the housing market fell that year, complicated financing was smoothed to such a degree that he even took Henry's land in trade for part of the price.

We left Manhattan the day after Thanksgiving. The day was sunny and warm, shirtsleeve weather. By the time we had loaded our Uhaul truck and stopped for supper in Greenfield it was dark and the temperature was dropping. We drove the final twenty-five miles to Heath, and found the plumber hadn't been able to hook up any heat or water and wouldn't be back til Monday.

Two sturdy teenage boys we knew helped all of us, including those three lovely girls, unload the truck. I found punky wood in the woodshed and built a fire in the stone fireplace. The boys then visited with us over cups of cocoa made on a camp stove and told us Heath Stories, about the weather and the Fair and farming disasters. Very cozy.

The boys soon left and went home to their cozy homes. The wind rattled the old windows and the temperature fell to ten degrees. We gathered up blankets and pillows to sleep in front of the fire, but it was less than cozy.

In the morning, Henry located and uncovered the dug well to haul up water for the three girls. We left them to do what sorting and unpacking they could while we drove to my mother's house in New Hampshire to get our stored furniture.

We again loaded up the Uhaul and that evening we all helped with the unloading, but we weren't done yet.

The next morning we set out in the Uhaul for a final trip to my mother's. My father had died that spring and my mother was visiting friends while she left the house in the care of a realtor. She had stored our stuff in her barn, and now it was our turn to store her stuff.

When we got home that third day and began to unpack the third truckload I asked Henry if we had arrived at Pork Corners. He staggered under the weight of a box of tools and grumbled that he didn't know, but this was the end of the road. We were never moving again.

We are literally at the end of the road. We do not have a driveway. We have a dirt road that ends in front of our house, where the plows and road graders turn around. Welcome to End of the Road Farm.

My First Farmgirl

Mabel Vreeland, our new next door neighbor, welcomed us to the neighborhood with a bushel basket of winter squash and parsnips from her garden. Mabel, who was eighty-two when we moved in, was a tiny woman with great spirit. Her younger brother Victor brought us a truckload of slabs for the woodstove. They recognized the need for fundamentals, food and fuel, but the most essential gift they gave was their friendship.

Like so many members of her family Mabel had cancer. When she was sixty the doctors said if she didn't have surgery she would be dead in six months. She said all her relatives had surgery and died anyway. She ignored the doctors, moved to an old family house on Knott Road and created her own healthy regimen. She planted an organic vegetable garden, drank purifying cornmeal water (a cup of cornmeal mixed with a quart of water and left to soak and settle), and parsley tea. By the time we met her the cancer had eaten away her nose which she kept covered with gauze, but this had not affected her stamina, strong will or good humor.

Even before we got to know Mabel we had a lot to thank her for. There were no other houses, and no power lines, on Knott Road when she moved here. Mabel was content to live without central heat, but she had electricity and phone lines brought in.

The community took care of her in that isolated spot as well as they could. The town plow made sure that the road was clear on the Sabbath so she could get to church in the winter. At the beginning of the bad weather Avery's General Store delivered her order – cases of canned vegetables so that if she got snowed in she would have a full larder.

Whenever I went down our hill to visit her she'd shake my hand with a firm grip. I'd always comment on that strong handshake and each time she would remind me that she used to milk six cows before breakfast when she was young.

Mabel needed more than strong hands during her life. Never marrying, she spent most of her working years in ministry to her Seventh Day Adventist church. She taught children, she worked at camp meetings, and most amazingly she served as lay pastor to three tiny churches in the Adirondacks for several years because no man would take on the job during the winter. She said, "I drove my car through the forest from one church to another singing hymns," (After she died we found a sign in her barn naming her as lay preacher in one of those churches. It is now a prized possession.)

She did a lot of hymn singing, driving through the winter woods, and paddling through river gorges in the summer with camp children. Later she sang in her own yard when the local congregation held occasional Sabbath services there because she was too frail to travel to church.

Mabel told us about our house which her two aunts, Edith and Emily, had lived in, adding what is now the main part of the building sometime around 1920. Mabel told us they were 'rich'. She also told us Aunt Edith died one winter when the snow was so deep, and so badly drifted that her body had to be brought from the house out to the main road on a toboggan.

With the slow arrival of spring I began to think about a vegetable garden. Mabel gave us the name of a man who could plow up the large garden I wanted, and encouraged me as I made plans. I asked how she managed her garden by herself when she had been so sick. She smiled and said, "Well, I go out to weed, and when I get tired I just take a nap on the path. When I'm ready I start to weed again." This was a good lesson in doing what you can as long as you can, without hurry or worry!

Victor came up just about every day to see Mabel and have lunch with her. Single all his life, he surprised her and all the neighbors by getting married when he retired. The marriage put paid to Mabel's idea that they would live together for their last years. Still he continued to see her every day and take care of chores around the house.

He didn't have Mabel's fire, but his blue eyes always had a twinkle. Like Mabel he was a devout Seventh Day Adventist, eating a vegetarian diet, keeping the Sabbath which is our Saturday, and never cursing.

However, whenever we met I gave the standard greeting, 'How are you?" He'd reply in a way that I never understood.

Finally, one day I asked Henry why Victor always replied, "Horny as ever!" with such a sweet smile. Well, Henry nearly fell over laughing. I had consistently been mis-hearing him. Victor, would never say such a thing. Victor was saying, "*Homely* as ever! *Homely* as ever!" With a smile.

Our first spring was long and cool with the last snow falling on April 16. We had made plans for the vegetable garden, but I was also determined to plant an old fashioned rose bush. During our last months in New York I spent a lot of time dreaming and reading about country life. One of those books, *Onward and Upward in the Garden* by Katherine White, had a beautiful garland of simple pink roses on the cover and praise for the Roses of Yesterday and Today nursery in California.

Mrs. White, as I always thought of her, did me a great service when she introduced me to Roses of Yesterday and Today because it was my introduction into a new world of romantic, but hardy roses. As Mrs. White suggested, the seductive prose in the catalog set my imagination reeling.

I read about *Belle de Crecy*, "one bloom with the fragrance to fill a room, and all the colors of the 'mad' gallicas," *Camaieux* with its candy cane stripes of pink white and red, *Celsiana* with "a crisp twirl of crinkled petals showing tall yellow stamens. True Damask fragrance," and *Rubrifolia* with its glaucus blue-red foliage and nearly black hips that was described as "singularly remindful of a Roman wall painting."

I was to acquire all these roses over time, but the rose I had to have first was the alba listed as *Maiden's Blush* with the French name *Cuisse de Nymphe* in parenthesis. The catalog said "Nature has created nothing more exquisite in plant or bloom than *Maiden's Blush*," but it was the translation from the French that caught me. *Cuisse de Nymphe* is *Passionate Nymph's Thigh*.

I sent my order off to Roses of Yesterday and Today, the passionate nymph arrived and was planted next to the front door in May. This was not a good decision, but it would take me a while to figure that out.

With our first rose planted, and the pastures surrounding the house greening up it was time for the arrival of 'young stock.' The two Hicks brothers who had a dairy farm down off the state highway, Route 2, brought their heifers up to our fields for summer pasture. The Hickses were always very careful about mending the fences, but one morning after Henry had gone off to work, and the girls to school, I looked out to see half a dozen heifers on the front lawn.

Now I had spent some years on a farm as a child. I had been friendly with cows. But when I saw those heifers on the lawn I panicked. I didn't know what to do. I called Mabel on the phone. I could hardly speak I was so agitated. While we talked I began to calm down and realized how ridiculous it was to ask for help from someone who was so ill. I apologized profusely and said the heifers and I would work it out.

I had nearly gotten all the heifers through the fence when Mabel came rushing up the hill, in her winter coat with a very proper Sunday go-to-meeting hat on her head, waving her broom.

I was embarrassed and full of apologies, but Mabel was not

distressed. We finished herding all the animals through the fence and propped it up in a very temporary way. Then we sat in the sun for a little while to collect ourselves. Mabel didn't want to go into the house. She said it made her sad to see the way the previous owner had knocked down walls and moved the kitchen.

After catching our breaths, I walked Mabel down the hill and made sure she had not harmed herself. That was the last time she ever made it up the hill.

Mabel failed slowly over the three years we knew her. Even when she was nearly bedridden herself, she made her morning phone calls to 'shut ins' to encourage them and bring them a little cheer. When she could no longer get up during winter nights to keep her wood stove going, she acquiesced in the installation of an electric heater and agreed to a Lifeline device that would call for help if there was an emergency. She refused to leave her house.

She died when she was eighty-five, as she had wished, in her own bed.

Mabel liked flowers and birds, but the garden she tended was strictly utilitarian. There was, and is, an enormous mock orange at the corner of the house that filled the air with perfume in spring, but she did not talk much about growing flowers.

One spring, sometime after she died, I was pruning the 'snowball tree' that grew at the corner of our house cutting back the winter's damage. There, under all the foliage and numerous snowballs, I found a beautiful little rose bush. It was petite, but obviously very hardy with lovely fragrance. I cleared away other plants to give it more room and air. I had no idea of its proper name, but it was obvious to me there was only one name I could give this rose. *Mabel.* She was my first Farm Girl rose.

A Rose Walk Grows

Having planted *Passionate Nymph's Thigh* from Roses of Yesterday and Today I could not stop. I was seduced not only by this one rose, but the romance of all the old antique roses, blooming in palace gardens, in cottage gardens, and in the great public gardens of another age.

I had no interest in the corseted scentless hybrid teas that needed so much coddling – and a good thing, too, because those roses are not hardy on my hillside where winter temperatures go below zero and bitter winds roar down our hill.

No, I was interested in big blowsy shrub roses that were fragrant and named after queens and noble ladies. I was beguiled by French and Latin names and by names that led to me check up on my British history. The *Rose of York and Lancaster* – what was that about?

I planted the Passionate Nymph next to the front door, with the idea that visitors could enjoy the fragrance when they knocked. There were two problems with this plan. First, no one ever uses this door because there is no path, only an uncomfortable slope in front of the house.

The second drawback is that this spot is right under the roof dripline, which isn't bad during the good weather, but during the winter icicles hang from the roof until they break off, knives and cudgels falling on the poor nymph. In spite of the battering, the Passionate Nymph survives, bent but unbowed, proving her stamina.

Soon I learned about the great Dr. Griffith Buck of Iowa State University and his cold hardy roses. I ordered *Applejack*, and planted it at the top of our road where it would welcome visitors just as the road began to curve bringing them to the front of the house.

Applejack is a tall graceful shrub with clusters of fragrant three or four inch pink flowers. It needs no winter protection and no sprays, only a little spring pruning to take out any of the inevitable winterkill. I do throw some compost around it every year, but I suspect our old border collie who died, and the two skunks that my husband fished out of a well who are now buried underneath it continue to provide it with good nourishment.

Since planting that first hardy Buck hybrid I have added the delicate pink *Quietness* and *Hawkeye Belle, Carefree Beauty* with its huge, bold pink blossoms, the pale yellow *Prairie Harvest* and the soft yellow-orange *Gentle Persuasion*.

Early on I came across a catalog from the High Country Roses that only sold roses for fall planting. I was intrigued and ordered four. When they arrived I was somewhat stunned to find four little sticks that looked like nothing at all, but I figured the nursery people knew what they were doing.

Since I did not know what I was doing I followed their instructions exactly. I do not remember at all why I chose the spot I did, but I dug a trench in the lawn, as directed, and put my four little sticks in it. I buried up my 'rose bushes' and even marked the spot properly.

In the spring I dug out the roses, or at least two of them. Two of the four seemed to have moldered away to nothing. No matter. I planted the two survivors. *De la Grifferai,* was the first, a small bush that produces lots of two inch tightly ruffled pink blooms. I later found that the great rosarian Peter Beales described it as vigorous but "rather coarse-foliaged" and "not of great garden value." He did allow that its vigor explained its presence in old gardens. Just right for Heath.

The other survivor was *Rosa rubrifolia* chosen because a catalog description of its blue-red foliage said that in the fall, with its nearly black hips, it looked like a Pompeian wall painting. That was almost as irresistible as the Passionate Nymph. It has grown into a tall (eight feet or so) vase shaped shrub with the promised unusual foliage and tiny pink flowers that are among the earliest on the Rose Walk.

Later, while I was visiting another beautiful garden, my hostess kept stopping to rip shoots out from between the flagstones of her path. She grumbled that the *Rosa rubrifolia* just sent shoots up everywhere. I was stunned. Mine didn't. Why not?

When I returned home I went to my rubrifolia and looked very carefully at the ground. There in the grass I could see dozens of tiny blue leaved seedlings. I had never noticed them because my husband who mows all around the roses which are planted in grass kept mowing them down. I took out my spade and dug up sections of sod containing these tiny seedlings, worked them out and planted them in pots. Through the years I have often done this. The seedlings grow quickly in the pot and make great presents for friends.

Rosa rubrifolia is now called *Rosa glauca,* the name still referring to the unusual color of the foliage. In spite of its unremarkable tiny flowers this is one of the most admired roses in the Rose Walk.

By the time winter arrived I realized that I had two roses planted in the lawn, with no logical reason for choosing that location. I thought I better come up with a reason that made some sense. After spending the winter looking at rose catalogs I ordered and planted eight new roses, thus beginning what I determined would be a Rose Walk. I imagined myself strolling between billowing rows of fragrant roses, wearing a big hat with trailing chiffon streamers.

After spring planting I now had six roses on one side of what would be a wide grass path and four on the other. I could see that anything recognizable as a Rose Walk would take a long time unless I planted more roses at a time. So I did.

By 1985 I had sixteen roses on the Walk and added nine more. The new rose bushes, *Madame Hardy, Ispahan, Comtesse de Murinais, Hawkeye Belle, Prairie Star, Therese Bugnet, Amiga Mia, Crested Moss*, and *Maytime*, were small and they bloomed modestly, but surely anyone with a little imagination could understand twenty-five roses arranged on either side of a path as a Rose Walk.

That June we invited a few neighbors over for Sunday afternoon tea, saying it was time to put away all those hectic spring chores. It was time to stop and smell the roses. I baked a cake, put on a rose printed dress and a straw hat and greeted my guests.

We did stroll and smell the roses. We exclaimed over their loveliness and hardiness. Our exclamations didn't take long, of course, but when we sat down for tea and cake the question was asked – is this the First Annual? Oh my, what a thought.

The idea remained at the back of my mind, but came to the fore when the new winter crop of rose catalogs arrived. Another half dozen roses were ordered.

Over the years I saw that certain rose families were hardier than others. The moss roses I planted died, and so did the damasks. However, the albas did well. *Alba semi-plena* with its single white blossoms and a center of golden stamens is somewhat lax in form, but it tolerates some shade which is a great benefit. The double *Madame Legras de St. Germain* and *Madame Plantier* are also white, but not all albas are in spite of the word 'alba' meaning 'white.' *Celestial* is a very double rich pink, as is the *Queen of Denmark. Felicite Parmentier* is a tall pale pink alba with amazing strength growing in the most difficult conditions in my garden.

The giant rugosa in front of the house, which I imagined was a beach rose brought home from a seaside vacation by the previous owners, inspired me to look at other rugosas. The three *Rugosa albas* I planted at the edge of the barn foundation grew thick, thorny and full of white blossoms in early June. *Blanc Double de Coubert* is a white rugosa often touted as a beauty for the garden. While I like it well enough, I don't think it holds a candle to *Mount Blanc* which grows more vigorously and floriferously for me.

Apart is a gorgeous pink rugosa that is probably as close to a cabbage rose as I will ever get. *Belle Poitvine*, full and pink, runs a close second right behind *Apart* in my affections. *Scabrosa* needs to be kept under firm control and *Dart's Dash* is not the deep deep color that was promised but it is beautiful, low and spready. It must be said the color of any flower can be affected somewhat by the difference in soil, moisture and temperature.

After our barn burned down in 1990, I started a Sunken Garden within the three stone walls of the foundation. I thought the walls would protect the roses from the winter wind that came roaring across our fields. I spent a couple of years building up the soil in the Sunken Garden before I decided I could finally try the more tender David Austin hybrids.

I planted the pink *Heritage*, the sunny yellow *Graham Thomas*, the dark and dusky red *Othello*, creamy white *Fair Bianca*, *Perdita*, the *Wife of Bath* and the buttery pink *Abraham Darby*. I felt I was putting all of English history and literature in the garden.

Alas, none of them survived long, but *Graham Thomas* and *Heritage* did their best. The soil was never very good in that spot. Stone foundations, like icebergs, are partially hidden making root growth difficult. Also, I had not anticipated the snow plow.

What people think of as our driveway is actually town road. This is a good thing because the town maintains it, including plowing in the winter. Since the road ends at our house, the plow has to turn around pushing the snow into great piles in the field, and to the south – over the edge of the foundation. The plow dumped tons of heavy snow and ice on those poor roses.

The second year, I did make frames to protect the roses, but between the extremely cold winter and the weight of all that snow, the roses could not recover sufficiently in the spring to thrive. They died.

Now I have only two Austin roses. *Mary Rose* honors King Henry VIII's flagship that sank 400 years ago but was finally found and lifted from its watery resting place just when Austin had a new rose in need of a name. *Mary Rose* is considered one of the very hardiest Austin roses. It is planted in the Shed Bed, next to the hen house, which presents its own problems. Next to *Mary Rose* is Austin's *Mrs. Doreen Pike*, a low growing shrub with an abundance of small pink roses that bloom all summer.

While the roses in the Shed Bed are somewhat sheltered from winter winds, they suffer from the affections of the hens who love to wander between the bushes to find the perfect spot for a dust bath. They think that well kept bed is intended for their personal beach. I have placed large-ish flat stones between the roses, but so far my attempts to keep the chickens at bay have met with mixed success.

Not all the roses bear the names of great ladies or moments in history. I also have what I call My Farmgirls.

I read about 'rose rustlers' those who went around searching in old cemeteries and old country gardens looking for beautiful roses whose names had been lost, but who retain the history of living in that spot for decades or even generations. I wanted to be a rose rustler, too.

When I let it be known that I was looking for endangered old roses a friend told me about a rose growing next to an abandoned house that was about to be demolished. My friend Fred and I went and dug up a piece and planted it by my pasture fence. It not only did well, it became invasive. After three or four years I had to dig it up and keep that area mowed until it was well and truly eradicated. That was the end of my career as a rose rustler, and the beginning of my career as a rose beggar.

There are a number of old farms in our town. Our gardens are a common topic of conversation so whenever anyone mentioned an ancient rose growing near their house, or in the garden I was not shy about asking if I might have a root some time. That is how I got *Alli's Pink* and *Terri's Pink*. After planting some other small bushes with pink blossoms I realized that women in town must have been sharing these roses long before I ever thought to ask. Then I appreciated the roses not only for themselves, but for what they said about friendship and generosity.

When I worked at the Buckland Library, one of the trustees with the greenest fingers I know gave me a root of a strong growing pink rose that she said grew everywhere in Buckland. She said some people called it *Belle Amour*, but since I already had a purchased *Belle Amour*, which it resembled not at all, I call it the *Buckland Rose*.

Actually the *Belle Amour* in my Shed Bed does not resemble the photograph of *Belle Amour* in Peter Beale's book Classic Roses either. This raises the whole issue of mis-named roses, which can come from a nursery as easily as not. My first experience with this was the arrival of a bush that produced gorgeous buttery pink double roses. I loved that rose. It seemed to glow from within. However, it was not the rose I ordered, which was the fuschia-red *Rose de Rescht*. No resemblance at all.

The problem with my misnamed rose is that when it died, and it did, I could not replace it. I later bought David Austin's *Abraham Darby* which came very close in appearance, but it also died. Twice. Some gardeners say they won't give up on a plant until they have killed it three times, so maybe I should give *Abraham Darby* another try. It grew so vigorously at my daughter's house in a slightly milder climate, that she ripped it out because it climbed too high and wide. I wish I had a problem like that.

Other masqueraders came bearing the names of *Rosa trigintepetala, Therese Bugnet, and Roserie de l'Hay*. I knew they were not what I ordered, but not what they were. Only one imposter, the so-called *trigintepetala* remains, spreading vigorously.

As I write this in 2011, I can count nearly 80 roses on the Rose Walk, along the pasture fence in back of the house, in the Shed

Bed next to the hen house, and on the new Rose Bank. I have to say that I have probably killed at least half that many. Each year when I go out to label the roses in preparation for the Annual Rose Viewing I find myself with a small handful of leftover labels.

Some of the roses never made it through one winter. Others survived many winters, but then slowly failed. When I look at my old records I sigh as I remember *Chapeau de Napoleon,* a crested moss; pink *Celsiana*, with it's gold centered fragrant blossoms that bloomed right at nose height; deep red *Robusta* which failed to live up to its name – twice. The candy striped *Camieux and Belle de Crecy*; a whole palace full of royals and their ladies – *Duchesse d'Angouleme, Duchesse de Verneuil,* icy white *Comtesse de Murinais, Madame Hardy, Marie de Blois, Constance Spry, Madame Isaac Pererire, Madame Zoetmans* and that queen of the kitchen, *Julia Child* – all died.

Even the men of history have not always survived on the Rose Walk. Gone are *Alexander McKenzie, Charles de Mills,* and *Cardinal Richelieu.* The beautiful scarlet *Champlain* barely hangs on, year after year.

And of course all the Austin hybrids were killed off by snow and cold in the Sunken Garden.

There is no doubt that I killed some of these roses myself, by improper planting. I always remember to plant peonies only an inch below the soil surface, but I do not dependably plant roses deep enough which is especially important in my climate.

Some roses died because they were simply not hardy enough. Some died for no reason I could identify.

The roses that survive do not do so because they receive any coddling. They grow in grass, which was not one of my better ideas, because the grass requires hand trimming. Every year or two I spread lime around the Rose Walks, now a double Walk, and the grass is as happy for this as the roses.

If I have compost left over in the late fall, which happens about half the time, I put a shovelful or two around each bush to act as protection as well as fertilizer.

I do no pruning in the fall, because there will inevitably be winterkill, and I want there to be as much growth as possible before the kill starts.

In the spring I prune out broken branches and winterkill. Sometimes it will be substantial. There have been years when the tall pink damask *Ispahan* has to be chopped down to less than half its size before it amazingly recovers to bloom as abundantly as ever.

I fertilize with compost tea or organic mixtures like Nature's Harvest, and try to keep them well watered if it is dry, at least up to the time of the Rose Viewing.

Since I am always buying, or otherwise acquiring, more roses than are dying, the Rose Walk has graduated from two long rows to three rows with two wide grass paths. One long row now extends along a pasture fence right to the Sunken Garden. I've planted other roses along a pasture fence in back of the house.

The Shed Bed next to our henhouse shelters *Belle Amour, Leda, Mrs. Doreen Pike* and *Mary Rose* from the worst of the wind. While sheltered from the wind, those roses do suffer from the hens who think that bed is their personal Lido for dust baths. I have tried various deterrents, but none have been very successful.

My latest project has been the Rose Bank. This area was re-graded after work on our house foundation. It seemed a perfect time to do something that would eliminate lawn that needed mowing. How could there be any answer but more of the very hardiest roses?

Mabel was the first rose on that bank, visible after hiding for several years, but other pink roses have joined her. The Purington family who have been farming Woodslawn Farm in a neighboring town for seven generations has given me several tough roses. *The Purington Rambler* has sent out tentacles that I think will be a great ground cover and the *Woodslawn Pink* is also growing strong. I think these three rugosas, *Pink Grootendorst, Dart's Dash,* a new *Therese Bugnet,* will spread and make a good groundcover, but I've also planted the pale pink *Hawkeye Belle,* and three *Double*

Red Knockout roses. Last summer I discovered a bit of the scarlet rugosa *Linda Campbell* among the weeds in the Sunken Garden. I transplanted her to the Rose Bank. The most recent additions are *Agnes*, a yellow rugosa, *Goldbusch*, a Kordes disease resistant hybrid, and *Gentle Persuasion*, a hardy deep apricot Buck hybrid

Knockouts don't carry the same romance as *Belle Poitvine* or the *Queen of Denmark*, but I can move with the times, and the *Knockouts* are tough roses.

History is not something that ends. History continues every day – and the Rose Walk and all the other roses at the End of the Road continue their history, living and dying, coming and going, but always during their sojourn giving delight.

Elsa

Mabel Vreeland encouraged us as we planted the altogether-too-big vegetable garden our first spring. At the same time we had begun reading the new *Shelburne Falls* and *West County News*, a biweekly newspaper that brought founder Mike Bakalar and his British wife Elsa into our lives. Elsa was the *West County News* garden columnist.

Henry and I both needed jobs and we soon found ourselves working for Mike and the *West County News* during our first summer. Elsa quickly snatched me away and I went to work for her at Greenfield Community College in the Continuing Education Division. It was my job to arrange non-credit workshops on office computer skills, miracles, nursing updates, self-hypnosis, dream interpretations and many other ordinary and arcane subjects including gardening. Elsa gave some of those gardening workshops in her famous garden on a Heath hill across town from us.

She also opened her garden to raise money for groups like the Friends of the Heath Free Public Library. Elsa admitted the garden was not to everyone's taste. She laughed when she told me about the time an austere and professorial neighbor, Ed, came up to visit. She said he took one look around at all the blooming perennials and said, "Ah, I see you are into gaudy" and he turned around and left. Ed's gardens of course were elegant and restrained, focused on a bed of various heaths (Ericaceae), with a tiny patch of lawn. The only ornament was a sundial surrounded by creeping thyme. His was a very different aesthetic and sense of humor.

Working with Elsa I became fascinated by a whole new set of garden terms and techniques -- perennials, biennials and annuals, not to mention double-digging, pegging down, pinching back and deadheading. Inspired by Elsa it was clear to me that I needed a perennial garden too.

Elsa started me off with divisions from her garden, plume poppy, *Campanula glomerata 'Joan Elliot,'* anthemis, feverfew, *'Miss Lingaard'* summer phlox, bee balm, and lady's mantle. Before I knew it, and while my husband shook his head, I had a ninety foot border filled with plants from Elsa, plant swaps, and occasionally from a nursery. It was never weeded sufficiently, partly because I often had trouble telling the difference between real weeds and the plants that self-seeded with abandon.

I learned more than garden techniques from Elsa. I also gained a new respect for the way different gardeners would create very different sorts of gardens, a perfect case in point being the professorial Ed. While she might laugh at his contemptuous exit, she did respect his right to have the kind of garden that would give him pleasure.

This was reassuring to me as a novice gardener, and as a gardener who eventually took a different road with my growing passion for roses. Roses did not interest Elsa very much, but she did have one beautiful blooming rose in her garden, *Queen Elizabeth*, chosen for obvious reasons. It was not dependably hardy in our climate, but she dependably replaced it every time it died out.

One year when her brother Peter was visiting from England and she was giving him a tour of the garden he stopped at her rose bush, frowned and asked what it was. Elsa looked at him in disbelief, "Why, it's *Queen Elizabeth*, of course."

In surprise he said, "Oh. I didn't know there was a dwarf variety."

Roses do grow differently, more austerely, in Heath than they do in England, or even down in the valley. But if we want a rose we will have a rose.

Since I had begun writing a garden column for *The Recorder* it was only a small leap to suggest to Elsa that she and I collaborate on a book together. Since Elsa preferred talking to writing this led to rambling interview sessions that were as much about her early life as about plants.

She told me stories about her life in England: about her flapper aunties; about the poorly set broken arm that developed gangrene and beloved Nonny who prevented an amputation and the long weeks in the hospital enduring salt water baths for her arm; about being a scholarship girl at Haberdashers' Aske's School for Girls; about Quarry Cottage where she lived while teaching at the Penshurst village school with over sixty students in her class; the children who presented her with jam jars full of tiddlers (tadpoles) as often as they brought her bouquets. During the Blitz many villagers went up to The Place, the great mansion in Penshurst, for shelter, but Elsa said she preferred staying in Quarry Cottage with her goats. She said they were quite used to being in the house.

I also remember her mentioning that one or two dashing servicemen found their way to her door in that perilous time. She was over sixty when I first met her and when I think of Elsa's charm then, I can only imagine what a dazzler she must have been at twenty-two.

I loved talking to Elsa about England and about her post-war days in New York City when she worked for the British Information Services. Because her skill as a public speaker who charmed as well as taught was recognized early on, she was often sent out to speak to groups about various aspects of life in England.

It was in New York that she met Mike Bakalar. Within a year they were married. They lived in an apartment in Greenwich Village and she told me that they wore out the kitchen linoleum dancing to Benny Goodman records.

Her stories about New York included tales of her years teaching English literature at Ethical Culture Fieldston School and the girls who spent their summers with her in Heath, waiting for Mike to join them on the weekends. The girls described those summers as camp for girls who didn't like camp. Elsa told a story of one visit to Tanglewood when a man passing by this gay group of girls asked what camp they were from. One of their number drew herself up and said they were *not* a camp. They were Mrs. Bakalar's girls!

The girls were devoted to Elsa and forbid anyone to find fault. One woman visiting Elsa's garden commented that the plants seemed awfully crowded. One of them was quick to interrupt her saying that Mrs. Bakalar was *not* into dirt! She was into *flowers!*

Some of those girls remained devoted until Elsa's very last days.

Our talks were so rambling that we finally decided to pick a topic and try to sell a short piece to a magazine, and note that we were writing a book. Since Elsa had so many opinions about the flaws of garden catalogs when describing color, and about how color and foliage forms could be used in the garden we launched ourselves into that topic. It took a couple of years, but the January 1987 issue of *Horticulture Magazine* featured Elsa amid her brilliant summer border on its cover.

During her years at GCC Elsa had also begun giving talks locally about her garden but between the time we began and the time 'The Flower Garden According to Elsa' was published

Elsa's lecturing career moved into high gear. After speaking at the Williamsburg Garden Symposium in the spring of 1986 and again in 1987 she was deluged with requests to speak all across the country, from the Whitney Museum in New York to Vancouver, Canada. Mike and his slides of the garden accompanied her everywhere.

Other noted gardeners, writers and photographers visited her gardens. Elsa once complained that this sort of work and fame came too late in her life, but it was just a token complaint as she and Mike hit the road again. When they stayed at home they started work on the book that would become *"A Garden of One's Own: Making and Keeping your Flower Garden* published in 1994. Elsa was quite definite about the subtitle. She would have no Design or Create. She insisted on those strong Anglo-Saxon words, Make and Keep.

It was a bit of a shock to learn that others had used the title "A Garden of One's Own," most notably Barbara Scott and Bobby Ward who edited a collection of Elizabeth Lawrence's writing. As Elsa learned, titles cannot be copyrighted, but it was vitally important to her to emphasize that a garden should first please the gardener, whether that meant gnomes in the shade, flaming perennials in the sun, or even a Rose Walk on a hill. If it pleased anyone else that was fine, but it was not the point of the garden.

Mike and Elsa were a team, able to work in tandem, but always allowing the other to follow his or her star. Elsa was willing to support Mike's dreams for the newspaper and Mike was willing to build stone walls for the garden, lie in the dew soaked lawn to take photographs at dawn, and once, to sit on the roof of the house with a 22 rifle waiting for the woodchuck who was ravaging Elsa's tall delphiniums. The woodchuck arrived and Mike took aim. He shot the delphinium dead. When he had climbed down to face Elsa he shrugged and said "It was its life or mine!" Elsa was willing to laugh.

When Mike died in 2000 Elsa's life changed rapidly. I took over driving and tech chores when Elsa went out on local speaking dates with her slides. She told me more and more stories about her childhood, about her parents, younger brother Peter, and beloved Nonny who lived with them and shared a room with Elsa for many years. During those rides it was clear that while she put on a good show for her audiences, she was failing. The Heath house with its gardens was sold.

Three young women, Mary, Susan and Eileen, who had taken workshops with Elsa, now came to help her tend a smaller garden in Ashfield. They were the Passionate Gardeners, planting and weeding alongside Elsa until that house and garden also had to be sold.

It was two of 'her girls,' former students, who became her honorary daughters, who helped manage her affairs in those last years. It was then I finally got to meet and work with those devoted and caring women, Marie and Nicole, who were such an important part of Elsa's mythic past.

Elsa passed away in January 2010. As I worked with Elsa's nephew Jake and his wife Susan, with Marie and Nicole, and with Susan, Mary and Eileen, the Passionate Gardeners, to organize a memorial service, I liked to think that I had become one of Mrs. Bakalar's girls, too.

The Annual Rose Viewing

If one has roses, one must have a garden party. And so we did. In 1985 I invited a few friends over on Sunday afternoon for a Rose Viewing. One guest, digging into her second piece of cake without giving a second glance at the few rose bushes in the lawn, said "You should do this every year."

On such slim threads as these are traditions born.

By the Second Annual Rose Viewing the gardening schedule was set, planting more roses, mowing, weeding and clipping all through June so that the lawn and roses would look their best. The first few years we scheduled the Rose Viewing for the Sunday closest to June 21, Midsummer's Eve. However, Heath remains cool well into June so even though the number of rose bushes continually increased the number of roses was never abundant.

We moved the ritual date to the last Sunday in June and were always happy when the last Sunday was late in the month. Once we tried the first weekend in July, but we ran into July Fourth celebrations when people had other commitments. Also, some of the rugosas were already fading. We went back to the last Sunday in June and there it remains.

The roses that have survived at the End of the Road are hardy and fragrant, but they do not bloom for a long season.

The rugosas begin blooming at the beginning of June, but by mid-July most of the roses, including the albas and gallicas, are done. Some consider this a flaw; I look at it like eating strawberries in season. The brevity of the season makes their loveliness and perfume that much more precious.

For some years we invited only friends and neighbors, but once I began mentioning the Rose Viewing in my garden column it seemed churlish not to invite others. Inspired by the British gardener and wit Beverley Nichols, I consider the Annual Rose Viewing my version of Garden Open Today and a general invitation goes out. Attendance varies. Sometimes my husband only has time to help people park their cars, filling up the back lawn. Other times the attendance is lighter and he has time to visit with our guests and tell stories of the roses from his point of view.

One friend expressed her admiration that I was so casual about inviting people to my garden. She said the stress of having so many people over would do her in. If she had said she couldn't believe how much of a showoff I was, I would have understood. I thought she knew me well enough to know that I am a good-enough girl. I leave perfectionism to others. I don't obsess about details. After all, when I invite guests to a dinner party I don't expect them to run their white gloves over the mantelpiece, or compare my dinner to a three star restaurant. Neither do I expect them to count the weeds in my country garden.

On the other hand if visitors do count the weeds, that is fine. There are two ways of enjoying a garden – or anything else in life. You can accept the pleasures offered; in the case of the Rose Viewing that is a lovely summer afternoon (it has never rained on the Rose Viewing – yet) blessed with perfumed Heath breezes, cookies and lemonade, and chats with other gardeners. If you want to count the weeds, or catalog flaws at any event, thinking that you could do much better, you will still leave happy, feeling pleasantly superior. I remind myself that either way I have given guests the opportunity to enjoy themselves.

I've made mistakes on the Rose Walk. I admit I have not always planted grafted roses deeply enough leading to their demise, and sometimes I've chosen roses that were too tender. But some mistakes live with me still. One was growing herbs and roses together which I found enchanting in a medieval sort of way. In addition I had read that tansy keeps away bugs. What better than an herb among the roses that would keep harmful bugs away.

Tansy is an attractive herb, growing about three feet tall with ferny foliage and button-like golden flowers that bloom long after the mostly pink and white roses. No need to worry about unpleasantly clashing color. but it did not take long to realize that tansy is extremely invasive. I still fight it on the Rose Walk, but it has also jumped into the field and even alongside our road. I think End of the Road Farm will have sufficient tansy til the end of time.

And so it was with mint. I must be the only person in the world who didn't know how invasive mint is. Now the mint and the tansy are battling it out in the field. I wonder who will win .

There have been other disasters. Twice we had serious fires. First, in 1990 our barn was struck by lightning and burned down on the Fourth of July. The heat was so intense it scorched the roses and trees as far away as one hundred yards. I was glad that the Rose Viewing had already been held, because I had to cut back all the damage. After this severe pruning the Rose Walk was not a lovely thing.

When all the burned barn debris was carted away we were left with three stone foundation walls - and the possibility of a Sunken Garden. Working in a garden we are never far from the reality of the cycles of life and death – and life again.

The second was a grass fire in the field around the Rose Walk. It was April and the ground still squished under our feet when we walked the field. My husband had a brush pile in the field and thought that since it was so wet he had a good opportunity for burning. He called Dispatch and got a burn permit, but he had barely gotten the fire going when the spring breeze picked up and carried the flame onto the dry grass that lay flattened over the wet ground.

By the time I got home from my Saturday rounds the last fire engine had just departed. The field was clear of brush- and sooty black. Fortunately the fire had stopped right at the barbed wire pasture fence that separated the Rose Walk from the field. On the rose side of the fence the lawn was mowed and there was no fuel. The leaf buds on the roses were just about breaking and were set back considerably, but soon new shoots showed that the roses had survived once again.

Some signs of the fire persisted at that year's Rose Viewing. One friend said she guessed the theme for the party was survival. I think survival is always the subtext.

Some people come to the Rose Viewing to find out how I keep bugs and disease from destroying my roses. They say they could never grow roses. "They are so much trouble. All that spraying and fussing. I couldn't do it," they say.

Well, I couldn't do it either. And I don't. The people who fear the trouble of caring for roses are usually thinking of hybrid teas and the kind of roses that they see in florist shops. Hybrid teas are beautiful, but they are tender and wouldn't survive our winters, even if I were willing to fuss.

There is now a group of roses that are labeled EarthKind. These are not hybrids, but a group of roses that have been tested by Texas A&M and found to be hardy and disease resistant. I think they are not only kind to the earth since they don't need poisons to thrive, they are also kind to the gardener who doesn't need to fuss with those things.

As more and more chemical poisons are outlawed, rose hybridizers are developing roses that are inherently disease and bug resistant. This is a good thing for the earth and for the gardener.

The single poison I have applied to the lawns near the raspberries and roses is Milky Spore Disease. It affects only the grubs in the lawn that turn into Japanese beetles. It is safe for all other wildlife and persists in the soil for years. I cannot say I have no Japanese beetles in my garden, but they are very few, easy to hand pick, and they only arrive after the Rose Viewing.

Once I named off the roses in the Sunken Garden for a visitor. He laughed and exclaimed that he had recently heard a story about old roses on the radio. The radio speaker said that his favorite was *Felicite Parmentier*, a tough alba rose with dozens of the palest pink, tightly furled petals and great fragrance. My visitor said he hadn't dared hope to see this rose – and there she was in all her glory. He was not disappointed.

Pleasure in a garden is reciprocal and circular. It is hard to know where being admired and being admiring begin and end. At a Garden Open Today the gardeners have their egos stroked, and the visitors have the pleasure of being in a garden where they are not responsible for the weeds. Enthusiasms and information are shared. The sun shines, and there is nothing for us all to do but stop and View the Roses.

Our Cottage Ornee

Our tax bill calls it a shed; some friends call it a camp; other friends call it a screened porch, but we call it our Cottage Ornee. According to my *Oxford Companion to Gardens* a Cottage Ornee is "a small, usually asymmetrically designed building containing elaborate rustic elements . . . used as a feature in a park, or as a lodge, or for housing. It is generally associated with the picturesque style in England."

We fail on all counts. Our cottage is perfectly symmetrical, a fifteen by fifteen foot square. It is certainly rustic but not elaborate, built with our own fingers out of local hemlock. Our son Chris helped with the tin roof and I occasionally helped with nailing on the siding, as well as holding the other end when necessary. It has no ornamentation. The unpainted wood reminds some people of summer camp.

On the other hand, if you consider our lawn and Rose Walk a 'park', the cottage is a feature of our landscape, tucked under an ancient apple. It is used for housing in the sense that Henry and I have slept out in the cottage when the house is full of boisterous family members. We also enjoy the cottage a deux, when we are resting from our garden labors, or when we break for teatime, or when we savor summer Sunday mornings with the newspaper, but we have also entertained people for luncheons, and dinners. Grandchildren have set out card games and Monopoly.

We've sheltered from the sun and rain. The tin roof crackles in the heat and plays a drummer's tattoo during a summer storm. It is small enough for comfortable solitude and large enough for welcoming hospitality

I have to say we once spent a riotous evening with a group of twenty-somethings in the cottage as darkness fell and the candles were lit. Books were brought out for some Reading Aloud, a children's book about Frida Kahlo read in Spanish, and a piece by Colette about her mother in the garden and a chapter of *archie and mehitabel* that literary cockroach and toujour gai cat. Laughter and literature. The evening ended when a visiting exchange student sent me into the house for the Bible and then gave a moving reading of Psalm 138 which includes the lines, "For the Lord, high as he is, cares for the lowly, and from afar he humbles the proud. Though I walk among foes, thou dost preserve my life, exerting thy power against the rage of my enemies and with thy right hand thou savest me." She read with such emotion that I wondered if she spoke of her own land, or how she felt in ours. An unforgettable evening.

Sometimes when people have helped bring the dinner dishes back into the house they suggest that we install electricity, a tiny kitchen and dish cabinets, but for me, the Cottage Ornee is Away. It is across the lawn and in view so it is not so far away that it is forgotten, but far enough away that all chores and to-do lists can be forgotten in its shelter. At least for a little while.

The cottage provides soft seating, and a table looking out over the Rose Walk and beyond to the field that we mow every year after the meadow birds have done nesting. When I take the tablecloth in for washing all necessary cleaning is done.

As simple a building as it is, it took us years just to decide that a fifteen foot square was the perfect size, small enough for solitude and large enough for society. Because we (which means

Henry) mostly built it with our own hands it took us another three years to build.

The first problem was the foundation. Our soil is rocky, especially in that spot where I had once tried to grow a long perennial border. I think the remains of a stone wall are there. It was impossible to dig holes for sono tubes by hand. Our friend Peter the Architect said it was perfectly legitimate to rest the building's four corners on giant boulders (which we had in plenty) in lieu of a conventional foundation and allow the building to 'float' in seasons of frost and thaw.

Our second problem was the roof. We wanted a low hip roof so that the building would sink into the landscape as much as possible, but we didn't understand how a hip roof was constructed. At a party I asked another architect friend how to make eight pieces of wood come together at the peak of the roof. He looked at me with some amusement. "We architects avoid having eight pieces of wood come together anywhere," he said gently.

With a little prompting from Peter the Architect we decided to use a pyramidal plexiglass skylight. That meant that we essentially built the roof from the top down. Henry built the frame for the skylight, after measuring it very very carefully. The day came when the roof was finished and it was time to install the skylight. We held our breath and then cheered as it slipped into place perfectly. "Why you'd think it was made for it," Henry said with a laugh.

The Cottage comes into its glory during The Annual Rose Viewing. After a stroll up and down the Rose Walk, the Cottage offers a soft seat and a cool refuge, as well as cookies and lemonade. And fresh strawberries.

The Cottage Ornee is just what the Annual Rose Viewing needed to be perfect.

Saint Fiacre Sat Here

Did you know, Saint Fiacre is considered the patron saint of gardeners? You can go to some garden centers and buy a statue of the good saint with his spade.

As it happens Saint Fiacre is also the patron saint of French taxi drivers. In Paris there is a large taxi rank outside the Church of Saint Fiacre. A slang term for French taxi drivers is "le fic", a colloquial reference to "figs" or that occupational hazard of taxi drivers – hemorrhoids. Inside the Church of Saint Fiacre is a stone bearing the imprint of the saint's bottom; sitting on this stone is said to cure that ailment.

One late June day my husband returned from working in the field shouting with excitement. "Wait til you see what I found!".

I was confused at the sight of a somewhat triangular concave boulder.

"Sit on it!" he ordered.

I sat and was comfortable because the concavities were so well shaped to my bottom, but still confused.

"Don't you see what this means? This means that St. Fiacre was here! He walked these Heathan hills and left his imprint for us gardeners just as he did for the French taxi drivers!"

I knew about the French taxi drivers and protested that we gardeners did not suffer from hemorrhoids.

"No, but we do suffer from a gardener's particular problem," he said lugging the stone to a log section I used as a stool. He set the rock on the log and sat me down on it. "Now, do you feel a cure taking place?"

I sat on the stone, my bottom tenderly supported and I looked around. The sky was an azure dome, birds were singing and turning somersaults in the air. The breezes were fragrant with the scent of my roses, blooming in shades of pink and white. The lawn, weedy patch though it was, was cool and green beneath my bare feet.

I sat in silence for a moment, then sighed. "I don't know what you mean about a cure, but just look at this perfect day," I said. "And I think the garden looks perfect, too."

"There you have it. You are cured of gardener's syndrome of never sitting to simply admire the beauty of the garden. You have put aside the spade and trowel, the lopper and pruners. You've ignored the weed, the beetle and aphid and admired the whole."

Well, I wasn't totally cured, of course, but I do sit periodically on the stone for booster shots.

Our own Saint Fiacre stone still sits in the Rose Walk. Visitors to the Rose Viewing sometimes sit on the saint's stone, or touch it, and we all ignore whatever tasks have been left undone. We stroll under the azure dome of sky, and inhale the breeze-borne scent of roses. We forget our chores, admire the beauty that we have cultivated and praise God.

Where the Blue Begins

Who can explain a horticultural passion?

My love for old fashioned roses began just before we moved to Heath in 1979. I owe my passion to Katherine White's book, *Onward and Upward in the Garden*, and her description of a rose catalog – not even the roses.

Katherine White was effusive about the Will Tillotson's Roses catalog. She enjoys his rhapsodic prose and quotes his description of one of his roses:

"OLD BLUSH. China. (1796) 4-5 feet, spreading. Not only 'The Last Rose of Summer' as immortalized by the poet Moore, but also the first and in between, for this China rose literally never stops. A semi-double 'fluttering assemblage of pink petals' giving an impression of airiness and gaiety. Don't plant it next to Chrysler Imperial (for instance) for 'never the twain' should meet."

Mrs. White describes Tillotson's catalog with a list, "the moss roses, the musk roses, the damasks and sweetbriers, the old fashioned hybrid teas and hardy perpetuals of my childhood …" and her delight ignited my passion for all those beauties who had never existed in my childhood. Not knowing anything about

Chrysler Imperial I imagined something bold and modern with none of the grace or romance that Will Tillotson called up in his descriptions.

I first learned about Edward Steichen (1879-1973), one of the most well known art photographers of the 20th century, noted for his dramatic black and white photographs, when I was fifteen and bought a copy of 'The Family of Man,' a book containing copies of the photographs that made up a monumental and moving exhibit at the Museum of Modern Art. Steichen was the Director of Photography at the MoMA and it was he who assembled the photographs depicting the emotions and needs that all people share across cultures and from birth to death.

Because of that book I got to know about Steichen and his own photographs and the Museum of Modern Art. In my initial youthful enthusiasm about his photography you might have thought I was the only person in the world to have discovered his talent, and the views he held of nature and humanity. When I did understand his place in the art world I felt I was clearly a smart and discriminating person, worthy of being in the company of other smart and discriminating people who had discovered him earlier. Before I was born.

When we lived in New York City I worked in one of the glass and steel towers on Sixth Avenue near the MoMA on West 53rd Street. I was able to nip over on my lunch hour to see the changing exhibits and wander around the gift shop where they sold a copy of one of Steichen's beautiful photos entitled 'Heavy Roses.'

I loved that photo but certainly never thought of Steichen as rose gardener or any other kind of flower gardener. That knowledge came to me much later.

In his 1986 book, *Farther Afield*, Alan Lacy describes his discovery of Steichen's passion for the delphinium. Lacy explains that Steichen was always an ardent gardener and early in the 1900s he became interested in genetics and plant breeding. He worked with cleomes, poppies and other flowers, as well as delphiniums which were his favorites.

Beginning in 1928 he began raising five acres of delphiniums at his home near West Redding, Connecticut. He once told a visitor, "This is where the blue begins." I can just imagine those five acres of blue, all bordered with the sunflowers he also hybridized. It must have been like looking at heaven spilled across the landscape, every shade and mood of the sky lit by a golden sun.

The delphinium is a magnificent plant with spires of blossom in every shade of blue from pale to royal as well as lavender, mauve, purple and cream. Sometimes their petals have an iridescent sheen. Catalogs give listings for Magic Fountain hybrids, Blackmore and Langdon Delphiniums, Pacific Giants and several other varieties. Sometimes the 'bee', the center of each flower is white or black or bicolored. They range in height from six or seven feet to bushier dwarf varieties that are only two feet tall.

Steichen was aware of the tendency of delphiniums to be knocked down in heavy spring rains and the necessity for artful staking. He had hybridized many of the tall delphiniums, but when he set to work to create what he would name the Connecticut Yankee delphium, he knew what he wanted - large flowers on a sturdy, bushy plant that would not be at the mercy of spring storms.

In the early 1960s he successfully created such a delphinium, Connecticut Yankee, one that would come true from seed. For Steichen the fun and satisfaction was in the creation. He was not in the nursery business so he gave the plant to a professional hybridizer, Frank Reinelt, who introduced it for sale in 1965.

In fact, besides learning about the birth of the Connecticut Yankee delphinium, Lacy learned that in 1936 Steichen persuaded the Museum of Modern Art to exhibit his delphiniums. He brought them in by the truckload and for one week, from June 24 to July 1, they were on display in those stark white halls. The show was a sensation: never since has MOMA devoted an exhibit to a live flower.

The New York Herald Tribune wrote that it was "the most amazing exhibit of delphiniums we have ever seen in this country by one man, one woman, or all men and women put together."

At that time the Museum of Modern Art was housed in an old townhouse on West 53rd Street in New York (the new building of steel and glass that I visited on my lunch hours was barely a dream), but its galleries usually exhibited the bright and thought provoking work of the modernists.

Think what New York must have been like in 1936. It was a hard time for many people. And yet summer does come to New York. The sun is high and shines more warmly down into the steel canyons. Fresh sea breezes blow off the harbor threading their way through the streets. But the city is a gray place, the blue sky so high and faraway that it is often forgotten.

Imagine what a stunning impression those delphiniums must have made on the New Yorkers of 1936. Surely the delphinium possesses more shades of rich and delicate blues than ever found their way to the palette of even the greatest painters.

I have been growing a clump of Connecticut Yankee delphiniums for several years, but it was not until I read Lacy's essay that I realized I had Steichen to thank for my own bit of heavenly blue.

We New England gardeners are fortunate that we can possess the same richness that Steichen enjoyed in West Redding, and that New Yorkers admired at the MoMA. The delphinium is a cool weather flower that thrives best in New England and the Pacific Northwest. It makes the winters worthwhile.

We can grow all manner of delphiniums, tall and short, in all the shades of summer skies. We can walk among them or cut them for our own domestic exhibit on the kitchen table. Outdoors or in, delphiniums give us a bit of heaven.

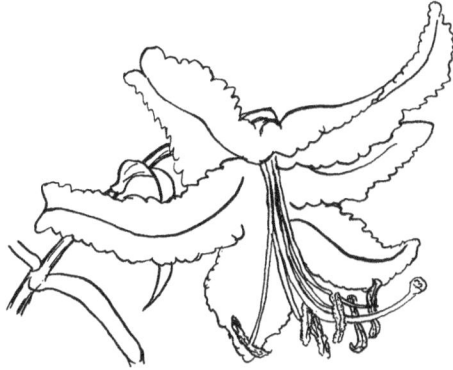

My Fragrant Garden

One of the main reasons I chose old fashioned roses was their hardiness. I knew this meant I had to give up repeat blooming, but what I got in addition to hardiness was fragrance. Most of the antique roses are deliciously fragrant. When a friend makes that instinctive movement of bringing her nose to a bouquet of my roses, she actually gets the fragrance she expected.

In his book, *The English Roses: Classic Favorites & New Selections*, David Austin talks about the fragrance of the old gallica, damask, and centifolia roses as well as the wild rugosas. He categorizes the variety of scent as the tea rose fragrance, myrhh, musk and fruit fragrances; explaining which of his hybrids have which variety of scent. Unfortunately, my nose is not that sensitive or analytical. I just know my roses smell wonderful. I do notice a difference in the intensity of the fragrance from year to year and wonder whether the cause is the amount of rain or the amount of sun, but I have no real explanation.

Since the roses have a relatively short season of bloom, and since fragrance has become important to me I have gradually added a number of other sweetly scented plants to the garden.

Our house came with the standard old lilac that is fragrant but not especially lovely and seems to go by very fast. However, there is also a grove of tall white lilacs growing at the east end of the house, blooming right outside the window of our 'office' on the second floor. It floods the room with fragrance enticing me to leave work and to play outside in the spring sun.

Once you have one or two lilacs it is hard not to want more. One year after visiting the Arnold Arboretum in Boston on Lilac Sunday I decided I had to have *Beauty of Moscow*. This is a double white lilac, but the delicately pink buds swell until they are fat and open into a white froth. *Miss Willmott,* another fragrant white lilac, came to me from my friend Jerry who has sixty lilacs as well as more than three hundred rhododendrons. I wanted this lilac not only for its beauty and scent but also because of its name. Ellen Willmott is one of the famous English gardeners of an earlier era. She is not as well known as Gertrude Jekyll, but I like to think she is not completely forgotten. Jerry also gave me the pink *Pocahantas*.

I planted the fragrant deep purple *Ludwig Spathe*, in a not very well considered site. It survives and blooms, behind the Cottage Ornee, but the spot is really too shady for the vigor I expected.

I wanted another pink lilac and planted *Miss Canada*. I like the name, the color, the great number of flowers and the late bloom season, but alas, she has no fragrance.

Although the perfume of lilacs and roses waft seasonally into the Cottage on Heath breezes, I wanted more fragrance. I had always loved the huge fountain of mock orange that grew at the corner of my neighbor Mabel's house. Twice I planted a mock orange at the corner of the Cottage, but they failed both times. Finally my friend Susan who has the greenest fingers of anyone I know, gave me a root from her shrub and it thrives. Now I have my own fountain of delicious mock orange blossoms.

Peonies can live undisturbed in one place for years, but over time I have transplanted mine in a kind of peony hedge. As I bought them I recorded most of their names in my intermittently kept journals, but now I would be hard pressed to say with certainty which are which.

Naturally my peony choices have been those varieties listed as fragrant, *Elsa Sass, Cora Stubbs, Lois E. Klehm* and *Mrs. Franklin D. Roosevelt* and others. I find that peonies have a subtle scent. To me it evokes a time when I lived in a farmhouse on the shore of Lake Champlain and my grandmother would bring in big bouquets of pink peonies. They filled my bedroom with their fresh scent. I don't actually have a strong memory of the peonies in the garden, but those lush pink bouquets on my dresser remain vivid.

When I went back to school at the University of Massachusetts, there was one place on campus that smelled heavenly in the summer even though there were no flowers in sight. Years later, when I met Dick Bonney, a master bee keeper, faculty member, and neighbor, I mentioned that mysterious fragrance, but said I didn't know where it came from. As it happened Dick had a map of all the trees on campus and he knew instantly what I had been smelling. Linden trees. Dick told me linden trees, also known as basswood or lime trees, were loved by bee keepers, because bees loved the flowers. When you enjoy a cup of delicate lime blossom tea, those blossoms come from the linden, not the citrusy lime tree. Linden flower honey is also considered very special.

Later, when Henry and I both worked at Williams College we admired another and younger lime tree walk on campus. That's when we decided we needed linden trees.

As former beekeepers we are always looking for ways to support honeybees which are so stressed by disease and mites. Linden trees were an obvious addition to our fragrant landscape. We invited children and grandchildren to the house for Memorial Day in 1990 to help plant some 'family trees.' I had six tiny linden whips (that's what you get when you are trying to be economical) for our three daughters and three granddaughters to plant. They went in along the pasture fence to the west of the house where we hoped that one day they would throw some shade on the house.

The tiny trees went in with great fanfare. They grew and grew. Two of them have survived but four died. Diane is our oldest daughter and her tree was the first to be damaged. The town plow snapped the trunk during a snowstorm. However, the tree didn't die, but showed its propensity to coppice, which is to send up many shoots when the main trunk is removed. It looks like a linden bush, but it continues to produce those fragrant flowers. We thought this was appropriate since Diane has four children, twice as many as her sisters. The most recent death was when a terrific windstorm ripped granddaughter Tricia's tree out by the roots.

Of course, any fragrant garden needs lilies. My big white oriental *Casa Blanca* lilies would look a bit more glamorous and mysterious if they had a little shade, but they are perfectly willing to strut their stuff in the sunny Lawn Bed.

Along the front of the piazza, in among the fragrant herbs I planted tall *Black Beauty* orienpet lilies with their graceful deep crimson recurved petals. Orienpets are a hybrid of oriental and trumpet lilies, making them more heat resistant and colorful than the plain orientals. The fragrance remains.

In honor of my husband I planted several Henry lilies. Henry's Lily *(L.henryi)* is an old variety with gold-orange recurved petals. I like the idea that this is a Chinese wildflower so it is another sort of souvenir of our days in Beijing. *White henryi* is – white, with a "starry heart of apricot and cinnamon," as the catalog says.

Lilies are usually too fragrant to bring into the house in a bouquet, but it is wonderful to be working out in the garden surrounded by that fragrance on a summer breeze.

I have many more fragrant flowers. Hyacinths, and some of the daffodils are fragrant in the spring. Sweet violets, lily of the valley, and iris bloom as the season progresses. Then come the roses, lilies and lavender, as well as summersweet, honeysuckle, sweet peas, and spicy dianthus. Some plants may not be especially beautiful, but once I had annual night scented stocks fill the evening air with sweetness I knew I needed to have them every year.

Gardens delight every sense. There is color and shape for the eyes, all manner of flavors for the mouth, texture for finger and cheek, birdsong and breeze for the ear, but the sense of smell is the most evocative. The scents of my garden carry me back to happy days of childhood, and deepen the romance I feel in my garden today.

Rachel's Rose

There is a rose in my garden named *Rachel*.

One summer Rachel Burrington Sumner, one of Heath's grand dames, who knew of my interest in old roses invited me to come to her house and dig up two of the roses growing there. She didn't know their names but thought I would love them as she did.

As I arrived I passed her two adult grandsons who were dashing off to a wedding, leaving Rachel and me in the big old farmhouse that had seen so much of life, so many weddings and births – and grieving, too. She gave me a tour of the farmhouse that she had come to as a bride. She explained all the work that her husband had done over the years before he died in 1988, and proudly pointed out the photographs of her children and grandchildren.

Then she took me outside to show me the roses which were no longer in bloom because it was so late in the season. Armed with my tough leather rose gloves and a shovel I set to work while Rachel returned to her chair in the kitchen.

It took me a while to dig up those roses. They were thorny and their roots went as deep and wide into the Heath soil as Rachel's did.

The rose growing in the front yard had spread into a large thicket and proved its indomitable hardiness. Rachel said during the excavation for a garage and workshop it had been buried under about three feet of soil. Rachel assumed the rose was lost forever, but in time it once again reached for the sun to spread and bloom.

I didn't know Rachel well. I didn't know her when she was a strong young woman taking her place in the community, working on the farm, raising a family and working down at the high school office. When I met her she was already becoming frail, yet still involved in the community. Whenever I had to arrange to use the church Rachel was the one I had to speak to.

Usually we only met at the Heath Fair. She'd ask about my garden and tell me about her pleasure in the season, in the new minister, in the latest town event.

After thanking Rachel I went home and planted both roses carefully. The summer and fall were very dry and even though I kept them watered as well as I could the roses took a beating. By the time winter was in sight I wondered whether those roses would survive.

Early in the spring I went out into my pasture collecting 'meadow muffins' and put the manure around Rachel's roses to they would get a good start on the season. Soon I could see there was new growth. They took hold.

It strikes me that the roses Rachel gave me are very like her – beautiful and strong. They have endured crushing blows and bloomed again. They'll flower and perfume the air no matter what, but they'll give pleasure to the people around them, as long as those people stop long enough, and are wise enough to notice.

My rose garden started with antique roses, often named after nobility, the Queen of Denmark, the Comtesse de Murinais and the Duchesse d'Angouleme.

I've been fortunate to have friends give me roses as a token of friendship. Most of these were unnamed so I tend to think of them in terms of the giver. Alli's Pink, Susan's Rose all grow in a row. Mrs. Herzig jumped the row and now grows by the roadside.

I think of these roses as my Farm Girls, but most of us women know that whether we are royalty or farm girls, we'd better be sturdy, tenacious and determined as we face the years of summer heat and winter storms or there will be nothing left of us to name a rose after.

I watched the new growth develop on Rachel's rose and hoped it would come along fast enough so that I could invite Rachel to see how well it had settled in and how happily it was blooming.

Rachel passed away before I had that opportunity, but I didn't admire the roses alone. Our youngest daughter, Kate, was married in the garden at the height of rose season. Family and friends joined us for this joyous celebration. We admired the bride and groom – and looked to the rose named Rachel for inspiration as they began their new life.

When it came time to build the Cottage Ornee we carefully sited it to nestle under the branches of the old apple tree at the edge of the lawn. We moved the four large boulders, salvaged from the barn fire, into position to hold the four main cottage supports. One of those boulders needed to be on the spot where we had planted Rachel's Rose.

There was no choice. We dug up Rachel's Rose and transplanted it to the top of the Rose Walk next to a low stone wall that grew out of what was left of the barn foundation.

Because I still wanted a rose in that spot when the Cottage was finished we planted the double pink alba *Celestial* next to the boulder. It thrived, and continues to bloom heavily every year.

But after a couple of years I noticed deeper pink roses among the more delicate *Celestial* blossoms. It was clear that we must have left a bit of Rachel's root in the soil when we moved her. Once again, as it had in Rachel Sumner's garden, this rose persevered until it reached through all obstacles to reach for and bloom in the sun once again.

Bonnie Kate's Wedding

Our daughter Kate was never much interested in the garden, but when I planted the first roses in 1980 and laid out the plan for the Rose Walk, she did express a romantic desire to be married amid the roses. On a June Sunday in 1994 it came to pass.

Like Adam and Eve who began their life in a garden, Kate and her beloved Greg stood with family and friends behind them, with roses and broccoli in front of them, and promised to be loving and faithful, in plenty and in want, in sickness and in health and in joy and in sorrow.

The minister, who is a friend and neighbor, asked the assembled guests if we would do what was necessary to support this new marriage.

Certainly many people had already done what they could to make the wedding beautiful. Neighbors had mowed the lawn, cleaned the house, brought barbecue grills and flowers and salmon mousse. Kate's siblings had built flower boxes, laid the stone terrace, trimmed and weeded and bought new clothes. So many people had promised aid and comfort – and they all delivered. No one forgot or failed. It was a miracle of love and generosity.

So having put hearts and hands to work for the wedding, we willingly pledged to support the marriage.

At least a few of the guests were experienced gardeners as well as experienced husbands and wives, and I expect they were already thinking of the supports that might be needed. Certainly newlyweds, like new gardeners, need encouragement along with a calming hand on the shoulder as the mysteries of growth unfold.

Gardens don't always turn out as expected. There are inexplicable failures. Seeds don't germinate, blight attacks the tomatoes, and delphiniums wither and die when you absolutely know you fertilized and staked just the way the book said.

Fortunately there are also those unexpected joys and bonuses. Cauliflower succeeds even though you heard it was really hard to grow, or an interesting sedum comes in on the root of the bee balm. Who knew it was there? Who knew such a pretty thing existed? Who knew it would love your soil?

Of course, each failure, each success, each surprise means the garden changes. Gardeners change. We lose interest in the cabbages, and develop a passion for squash.

We love fancy jam and decide to grow fancy berries. We decide dahlias are vulgar and devote ourselves to dwarf conifers.

Perhaps most amazing of all, we realize that there is always something new to marvel at and enjoy. Suddenly we see that the garden is not only color and fragrance, we become aware of the garden sounds: the wind rattling the bamboo, the deep thrum of the August cicada. It may have been there all the time, but we never noticed, or gave thanks.

Happy the spouse who can watch with delight as new passions, new skills and talents emerge, even as some loved habits and thoughts fall away.

It rained all week before the wedding. Saturday the skies were dark, but dry. At the appointed hour and preceded by her sisters, Kate entered the wedding tent. Just as her train cleared the tent the skies opened. Torrents fell and the assemblage laughed. When it was time for the bride and groom to take their vows the rain stopped – just as suddenly as it began. Greg and Kate stepped out into the dazzling sunlight promising to love and honor each other forever.

A few minutes later, while the photographer was busily snapping away, heavy mists blew across the hillside. The view disappeared. We couldn't see across the pasture any more than we could see into the future. There was only romance and the scent of rain-splashed roses.

At such a moment it's easy to imagine plenty and health and joy. After all who sets out the tomato plants without picturing the abundant harvest of red fruit that delights the eye, pleases the palate and satisfies the belly? But as Adam and Eve found in that first garden there can be trouble as well.

Gardeners spend a lot of time on their knees, in careful observation, in grubby and tedious weeding, in setting out slug traps, in admiration, in supplication, in gratitude. As a wife I've spent a few hours on my knees, weeping, praying, cursing – and giving thanks for my great good fortune.

In the garden there are beautiful roses, fragrant herbs, tender lettuces, nourishing beans – but lurking in the soil and air are slugs and bugs, beetles, wilt and blight. The garden is not carefree. And yet, the slimy slug is just as inevitable in the healthy garden as the singing bird. Sun and rain. Brilliant day and darkest night. All inevitable. All necessary.

And so as Henry and I watched our bonnie Kate and beloved Greg step into a new space to make a garden of their own, we tucked our prayerful wishes into their tool basket. Wishes for strength and patience and joy.

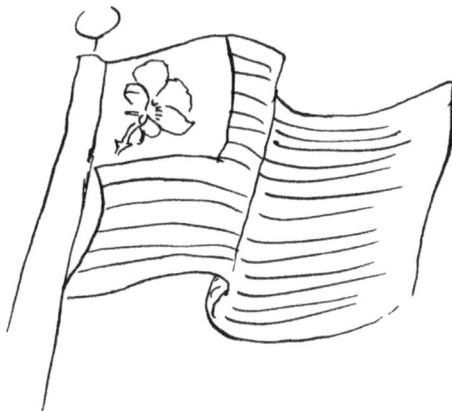

The Rose - Our National Flower

The rose is a flower that grows all over the world. It is so beautiful and so varied in form that it is no surprise that many countries including England, Bulgaria, the Czech Republic, Slovakia, and Ecuador, have chosen it as their national symbol. It is also the national flower of Iran where it has grown for centuries, and was carried to the west by Alexander the Great. In 1986, after many other flowers including the marigold were considered, the rose was declared the national flower of the United States.

Whatever your favorite - a beach rose or a ramblin' rose – a tea, floribunda, grandiflora, hybrid or old rose - *Queen Elizabeth*, *Christian Dior* or *Mr. Lincoln* - the national rose is The Rose, and you can take your pick.

Once, when the Florist Transworld Delivery (FTD) surveyed their customers, most named the rose as their favorite flower.

Maybe one of the reasons that roses are such a popular cut flower is that they convey such a variety of messages in the language of flowers. We all know that red roses say "I love you," but white roses stand for innocence and purity, yellow roses for joy and pale pink roses for admiration. They are also suitable for any celebratory occasion.

Roses have a very long history in our country. Fossilized rose petals, estimated to have bloomed thirty-five million years ago, have been found in Montana and Oregon. Roses still bloom in every one of our 50 states.

On October 11, 1492, when they were ready to turn back, Columbus' sailors picked up a rose bush floating in the sea and gained the courage to continue on.

The pilgrims planted roses in 1621 and George Washington, our first president, raised roses at Mount Vernon, as did Thomas Jefferson at Monticello. William Penn was very fond of the rose. He brought eighteen rose bushes back to this country after a trip abroad in 1699. Later, beginning in 1731, his family rented parcels of land for the annual payment of one red rose.

The rose appeared on our early currency. A five petalled rose was placed in the center of a 1722 coin, and cupids and wreaths of roses adorn a three dollar bill dated 1856.

We've even had a president named after the rose; Roosevelt means 'field of roses.'

Ever since it was planted in 1913 under the direction of Mrs. Woodrow Wilson many ceremonial events take place in the Rose Garden at the White House.

In addition to Mr. Lincoln, other presidents and their ladies have had roses named after them. *The John F. Kennedy* rose is a hardy white hybrid tea; *Herbert Hoover* is an orange, gold and deep pink hybrid tea; and *Pat Nixon* is a deep red rose. *Rosalynn Carter* has always had a rose in her name long before a brilliant scarlet rose was named after her. *Nancy Reagan* has been honored with an apricot hybrid tea.

Solemn ceremonies held at the Tomb of the Unknown Soldier often include bouquets and wreaths of roses.

If we remember our war dead with roses, we have also celebrated peace with roses. One of the most popular roses of the 20th century was developed in 1942 by the French hybridizer Francis Meilland. Just before France fell to the Germans, a piece of the budwood was brought out of France and carried to the

U.S. where the Conrad Pyle Nursery propagated it. It was named *Peace* in hope, and, by happy chance, it was introduced to the market on VE day, the day Berlin fell.

On the day that the war ended in Japan, in August of 1945, the *Peace* rose was named an All America Rose Selection, the only rose so designated that year. On the day we signed The Treaty of Peace with Japan, that officially ended the war on September 8, 1951, the American Rose Society awarded its first gold medal to *Peace*.

Many roses have immigrated to our shores over the years and it seems to me that there is a special symbolism about choosing the rose as our national flower . We are a nation of immigrants. Rose varieties from all over the world have come here, and been crossed and recrossed to come up with some of the most beautiful modern roses.

When I think about the history of the rose in our own country, and look at my *Rosa setigira* , a native climbing rose, I can think of my Rose Walk as not only hardy, practical, romantic, beautiful and fragrant, I can also think of it as patriotic.

The Road to Beijing

I have made leaps in my life, but surely one of the longest was the leap from Heath to Beijing.

In 1988 I was preparing to leave my post at Greenfield Community College when a colleague made a suggestion. "You ought to take Marguerite's job in China."

Nearly a year earlier Marguerite had begun a stint as a 'Foreign Expert' with *Women of China Magazine* which operated under the auspices of the All China Women's Federation. This magazine, published in English, distributed internationally but not in China, gave an honest report of Chinese women's current lives. Marguerite acted as a 'polisher' charged with making sure that the English translations of Chinese interviews and articles were correct in every way. Her contract was coming to an end and she was helping the *Women of China* work unit find a replacement.

After a remarkably brief period of discussion with my husband we decided to apply for the position. Henry doesn't enjoy being a tourist, but the idea of living and working in another country, any country, for an extended period of time was appealing.

In the end it took over a year to make the arrangements. Sometimes letters said they needed me immediately but months of silence followed. Then, when we had given up all hope that this adventure would ever begin, there was a rush of phone calls, telegrams, requests for more medical records – "Send syphilis soonest!" – and directions for getting our visas in New York City.

We found renters for our house, got shots for hepatitis and typhoid, gave our cats to daughter Betsy, and set off on a new adventure.

We left on April 16, 1989. Unbeknownst to us this was the day following the death of Communist reformer and champion of university students Hu Yaobang. Already students were gathering in Tiananmen Square to mourn their hero– and to set in motion the Beijing Spring and the events that culminated in the Tiananmen Massacre.

We landed in Beijing in the middle of the night, after traveling for twenty-two hours. Excited young representatives from the magazine, some of the translators I would be working with, met us with solicitous inquiries about our health and state of exhaustion.

We piled into a small van with our luggage and drove through what we came to recognize as Beijing murk. Streets were dark, streetlights were rare and new skyscrapers were only darker shadows against a dark sky. The air was filled with Beijing dust carried by the spring winds. We soon understood why so many people wore old fashioned surgical masks or wrapped their heads in pretty chiffon scarves.

An hour later we arrived at our destination, the Friendship Hotel where a small apartment had been assigned to us. The neon lights and small palms outside the registration office made me feel I was in a Charlie Chan movie. Of course, I was slightly drunk with exhaustion at this point.

At the registration desk the hotel staff started to giggle. Our room was number 8741 which is to say ba-qi-si-yi (ba-chee-suh-yee) which was close enough to Pa-tree-see-ah for the pun loving Chinese to be very amused.

My new colleagues chatted with us all the way to Building Eight, but at the main door I hesitated. "Listen. What is that sound?" I was hearing the faintest mysterious melody that only added to my Charlie Chan hallucination.

"Oh, that is the students chanting in Tiananmen Square," one translator answered. That was our introduction to the long and complex history and culture of China.

Our first five weeks in Beijing were thrilling. The student gathering quickly changed from a demonstration of respect for Hu Yaobang to a demonstration for we-knew-not-quite what. Every day we had lunch in the Foreign Experts Dining Hall and the conversation among the professors, journalists and various flavors of old China hands was all about the latest developments in Tiananmen Square, the latest rumors, what was left out of the latest official news reports and speculation about what all those rumors and reports meant. When Henry or I asked for clarification on some point the first response was always, "Well, it's very complicated."

My work unit was excited about the possibility that beneficial changes might be in the offing. Even when the army was called in, my colleagues were unworried. The People's Army would never harm the people they said. They quoted a phrase of Mao Zedong's that said the people were water and the army was fish. Fish cannot harm the water.

As the Chinese and the world learned, that phrase lost its credibility in the early hours of Sunday, June 4 as tanks rolled into Tiananmen, killing an unknown number of students and putting an end to the hopefulness of the Beijing Spring.

In spite of what my colleagues called 'the turmoil,' our life as Foreign Experts settled down to a quiet routine. The work load was not onerous and we had lots of time to ride our newly acquired bicycles around the city and to begin learning about China and its 5,000 year history.

In 1989 there were no privately owned cars in Beijing. All motor vehicles belonged to work units. Bicycles were the major mode of transportation. People bicycled to work, to run errands, to visit, and to move goods and produce around the city. While we bicycled the ancient streets of Beijing, we could also see modern office towers rising above us and crowded with power cranes, humorously referred to as the national bird of China.

To accommodate bicycle and vehicular traffic, the broad roads were divided into three sections with wide bike paths on either side of a lane for vehicular traffic. Those lanes were divided by medians planted with trees and pink roses.

One of the articles I had to polish for *Women of China* mentioned 'monthly roses.' In my ignorance I thought this was a bad translation and we had quite a go round about it as I tried to find a better phrase. In fact 'monthly rose' is a descriptive phrase that I run into occasionally, even now, in English language garden books when referring to the reblooming, or remontant, roses that were brought from China as early as the mid-1700s. Until horticulturists began using the 'China rose' for hybridizing, roses only bloomed for a short season. All the 'everblooming' roses of today have the China rose to thank for their long season.

The single pink roses growing in the roadway meridians did not resemble what I knew about tender 'China roses' with double blossoms on what were often large shrubs, but they were almost the only roses we saw during our time in Beijing.

Though we saw few roses, we did have a chance to see some of the great Chinese gardens before we left in the spring of 1990. One of my colleagues accompanied us as guide and translator to Hangzhou, known for its natural beauties, and then Suzhou where his family lived.

In Hangzhou we visited the great Lingyin Temple. The entry is by Feilai Peak, or Flying Mountain, carved with hundreds of

Buddhas. The story is that a Buddhist monk came upon this limestone mountain and exclaimed that it must have flown all the way from India, it was so different from the surrounding sandstone mountains. We were particularly taken with the largest of the Buddhas known as the Buddha of Joy.

Suzhou is sometimes known as the Venice of China because of its extensive system of canals but it is also famous for its ancient classical gardens, many of which have been restored in recent years.

We toured several of those gardens including the wonderfully named Humble Administrator's Garden. This grand ten acre garden, enclosed by walls, of course, included a large pond and streams, woodlands, bamboo and forty-eight pavilions and buildings with poetic names like Celestial Spring Pavilion or Hall of Distant Fragrance.

A very different garden is the Lion Grove Garden, famous for its rockeries of Lake Tai eroded limestone, much prized in the Chinese garden for its 'ugliness.' I didn't even want to take the time to visit this garden because the description was all about the stone. I had started to understand that Chinese gardens were not mainly about flowers, but a garden of stone held very little appeal.

Still, I am glad we went because it was so much fun to see the Chinese tourists in this garden, climbing the rocky 'mountains,' hiding in the caves and grottoes, winding through the labyrinth, laughing and having as much fun as any American tourist at an amusement park.

The garden that touched my imagination was the Master of the Nets garden, Wang Shi Yuan, the smallest (one and a third acres) of these classical gardens. By the time we prepared to leave China I had come to think the life of the Chinese scholar was ideal: writing, reading, gardening, with good food and social gatherings in the evening. The Master of the Nets is what I think of as the quintessential scholar's garden, hinting at this ideal. We will not think about what it took to support such a life.

Like all the classical gardens, the Master of the Nets is designed to balance the yin and yang of water and stone. The dark, soft, cool moistness of yin must be balanced with the bright, hard, dry heat of yang. Sculptural rocks and paving are elements suggesting the natural mountain landscape while water offers the contrasting sense of refreshment.

Ideally gardens are arranged to subtly impress the visitor with the passage of time – the fleeting moments it takes a leaf to float down a stream or disappear under a bridge to reappear a moment later, or the shifting of shadows as day moves towards its close.

The progression of the year is suggested by seasonal plantings, narcissus and peonies in the spring, orchids in the summer, chrysanthemums in autumn and the plum blossoms in winter. Formal paved courtyards are often adorned with these handsomely potted plants. Longer epochs of time show in the maturing growth of a tree, the lichen gathering on stone or the patina on bronze.

The pond at Wang Shi Yuan is surrounded by curving paths and pavilions including the small Pavilion Welcoming The Advent of the Moon and Breezes. It's easy to imagine a select group of scholars (no women) sitting there on a summer evening, drinking, reading poetry, gazing at the reflection of the stars in the water, and possibly thinking of themselves as fishermen. The name of this garden was inspired by the old saying, "right and wrong reach not where men fish; glory and disgrace dog the official riding his horse."

This is another version of the strong tradition of the wise government official who finally chooses the poverty and freedom of the mountainside and a garden of chrysanthemums over the constraints of holding office.

To one side of the pond is the Late Spring Studio, designed with a covered moon viewing terrace, a small half pavilion named Cold Spring Pavilion for the spring that bubbles out of the rock next to it, arrangements of Tai Hu stone and gray terracotta paving and balustrades. The plantings are spare and elegant.

This courtyard complete with its moon gate has been recreated at the Metropolitan Museum of Art in New York City and named Astor Court in honor of Brooke Astor, a Museum trustee. Mrs. Astor had spent part of her childhood in Beijing and learned to love the serenity of the Chinese garden. Recreating this courtyard at the Metropolitan was a major collaboration between the Chinese government and the Museum. All the materials and parts of the courtyard were duplicated in China, then shipped to New York along with a crew of craftsmen who assembled it all under a large skylight.

Not long before we returned home I met a professor at a meeting and he told me how lonely he had been during a long academic sojourn in New York in the 80s. Nothing was familiar - not the traffic, or the enormous skyscrapers, not the clothes and not the food. But one day he found his way to the Metropolitan Museum and the Astor Court. With a deep sigh he said it was as though he was magically transported back to China. It was exactly like home.

Later, on my own trip to New York I visited the Astor Court and I knew just what he meant. Like the Flying Mountain with its Buddha of Joy I had soared back to Suzhou. It was not only the authenticity of the materials and design, it was the quality of light. While I cannot imagine myself in the heat of Egypt when I visit the Metropolitan's Temple of Dendur exhibit, when I sat under the skylight in Astor Court I too was transported to a garden beneath the gray skies of China, transported to memories of an extraordinary adventure.

When we returned to the End of the Road I rushed to see the spring growth in the ninety foot long perennial bed I had been planting and tending under the inspiration and tutelage of my friend, Elsa Bakalar. What I saw was a mass of weeds. Weeding has never been my strong suit, and this long border was always beyond my capabilities. Now it was essentially gone.

However, as I mourned the loss of this bed with its coreopsis, foxglove, marguerites, plume poppies, campanulas, and all the plants from plant swaps as well as from Elsa's garden, I began to see that this was an opportunity to think about a different kind of garden.

As part of our homecoming after our second year in China which included attendance at the United Nations Women's Conference I was asked to give a 'sermon' about our trip at a local church. I concluded my comments with one of the Chinese philosopher's Chuang Tzu stories that I had heard during our first stay. Once there was a frog who lived in a well and thought he knew all there was to know about the world. But one day he managed to hop to the top of the well and when faced with the immensity of the ocean and the sky he realized he knew nothing.

Afterwards one of my friends said he came expecting a report on the women's conference, but was surprised to get a disquisition on the nature of knowledge instead. I don't think this was an especially positive remark, but when I think of my time in China and my limited understanding of China's history and culture, even in such a small area as its gardens, I feel just like that frog confronted by the ocean and sky for the first time.

So as I stood and looked at the ruin of my English perennial border, I thought about the Chinese gardens which only appear to have a simpler aesthetic with a more limited palette of flowers. I knew that I, a little frog, certainly couldn't create a classic Chinese garden, but I was ready to begin from a new vantage point.

Lightning Strikes

After spending a year working in Beijing, China, from April 1989 to April 1990, we returned to the End of the Road.

It was wonderful to arrive in time to see what we needed to do to set the garden to rights. A garden is an ephemeral thing and even a year without care can destroy it. The vegetable garden was our first priority, but the 90 foot perennial border I had been building under the inspiration of Elsa was a lost cause. Self seeders had spread everywhere and were all interspersed with weeds. Fortunately I had brought a new garden vision , stone and water, home with me from China. I gave up the perennials, for the moment, while I reconsidered the flowery aspects of my garden.

The Rose Walk had not suffered during our absence, at least no more than usual and it was a pleasure to stroll along the walk and take out the bits of winterkill, knowing that the roses would bloom as fragrantly as usual.

We organized our tools in the barn and set to work, never imagining that a big change was coming.

Our barn was a remnant of the time when our land was a real farm. It had three stories and a long and useful history, but by the time we acquired it the cattle and sheep were gone, as was most of the hay and farm equipment. The barn only stored lawn mowers, tools and the odd equipment that accumulates around any home. At 2 a.m. on July 5th its usefulness, even as an oversized tool and garden shed ended. Lightning struck.

The Fourth of July had been hot. Sultry. There was a barbecue with neighbors, and a few firecrackers, but no one had much energy. When we got home we opened all the windows, closed during the day to keep out the heat, and hoped for a few of our famed Heath breezes to find their way in. We went to bed as we heard far off rumbles of thunder.

We slept through the first part of the storm, but a deafening crack of thunder sent my husband Henry toward the open window where the rain was blowing in. Before he could cross the floor there was a second thunderclap. He jumped back in bed and said he'd wait. The third thunderclap shook the house. Then he asked me if I smelled ozone. I said I smelled smoke.

This time the continuing thunder didn't stop him. He looked out the window. "The barn's on fire!".

We had electricity but lightning had also hit the telephone pole disabling our phone. Henry pulled on his pants, jumped into the car, parked right next to the burning barn and drove to the bottom of the hill, blaring the horn all the way to wake our neighbor, David. His mouth was so dry from fear that by the time David opened the door to him, he could not even speak until he had taken a drink of water. Then he telephoned the fire department.

The first members of the Heath Volunteer Fire Department arrived within fifteen minutes; by that time the barn was totally engulfed in flames and our house, only sixty-five feet away, was beginning to smoke.

The firemen started to hose down the house. My husband stuffed me into the car and drove me down to our neighbor warning me that we might lose the house. I had been so stunned by the sight of the enormous blaze that I never even thought about what I should save – the family photos, my computer disks or my "jewels," such as they were. I had wandered around the kitchen wondering when I should start making coffee for the firemen.

I waited with my neighbor Dorothy and we talked while we watched more fire engines, now from Rowe, Charlemont, Colrain and Shelburne Falls go up the road.

By 3 o'clock I needed to leave Dorothy. I understood that Henry didn't want me to watch our worldly goods go up in smoke, but I needed to be back up the hill. I passed Henry who was helping the firemen set up pumps and hoses at the Frog Pond. That pond had actually been built as a fire pond in the field below our house, but we never imagined it would be used for anything but newt catching with the grandchildren.

By the time I got to the front lawn, the barn had fallen in on itself; a slight breeze was blowing from the west. The house was safe. The sounds of the burning barn and the crackling static on the firemen's walkie talkies as they coordinated between the pumpers and the crew at the pond were almost lost in the immensity of the night.

The flames threw exaggerated shadows on the figures moving hoses around the barn, across the lawn and along the road. My eyes stung from the smoke and only gradually did I recognize the faces of the selectmen, the teacher, the minister, the farmer, the father with his sons as they labored. These were my neighbors. They nodded at me as they worked but never broke their concentration on the job at hand. There was no conversation. There was no time. Besides what can you say to the people who are saving the substance of your life.

There were many faces that I didn't recognize, and yet these were my neighbors, too. They were not my friends. How could they be? We had never met and did not know each other. They lived in surrounding towns and still they had tumbled out of bed in the middle of the night without a second thought to come to my aid because they were my neighbors.

The sky lightened and I felt the dawn chill. The sweltering

temperatures of the Fourth had dissipated and the inferno that had been the barn was cooling. One by one the firemen and equipment of the other towns drove off, never waiting for a thank you. We drank coffee and juice with the other firemen, brought by the firemen's wives, and the talk started – of other storms and other fires. One young man asked my husband if we made our living with the barn. When the answer was no the young man acknowledged solemnly that we were fortunate.

There was no more threat to us, but behind the eyes and calm faces I could see the memory of other barn fires when life and livelihood had been lost.

The next day when a friend called to say she had just heard about the fire she said I was awfully unlucky. First "counter-revolutionary rebellion" that made headlines worldwide during our stay in Beijing, and now the barn fire. But she's wrong of course. I am one of the luckiest people I know and the major part of my good fortune lies in living where I am surrounded by neighbors, people who don't know me but buoy me up in time of trouble. I can't begin to thank these neighbors except by being a neighbor myself, and I hope I will always be up to the task.

The barn is history. A neighbor told me it had probably been cobbled from the timbers of several other barns; that was the way barns used to continue beyond their own lifetimes. After the fire only the stone foundation was left, but already new visions were dancing in my mind – perhaps a sunken garden where tender David Austin roses could be sheltered.

I walked down the Rose Walk, to see how the roses had survived. They were singed, and even burned from the intense heat of the fire. I could not gauge how severe the damage was. Most of the roses had come through frigid winters, but could they also survive an inferno? We would see.

I can never work in the garden without thinking of death and rebirth, but the Rose Walk will always be especially suited for contemplating destruction and renewal. The cycle of life.

Constance and Charlotte

I once saw a full page florist ad with a profusion of gourds, pumpkins, artichokes, millet, wheat, kale, sage and Indian corn arranged with roses, mums, daisies, miniature calla lilies and waterlily. The arrangements were lovely. Any of us would have been happy to put such centerpieces on our Thanksgiving table.

Very pretty. Definitely not shocking. But shock is what greeted Constance Spry's outrageous arrangements in the Britain of the 1920s and 30s. She was possibly the first to break down the barriers that existed between the flower garden and the kitchen garden. I think we can credit Constance Spry with many of the ways we use and decorate with flowers today.

Constance Spry is not a household name. Certainly not to Americans, not even American gardeners, although those rose lovers among us may have noticed that David Austin, the great British rosarian and hybridizer, named the first of his English roses after her. But there was a time when this woman, who opened a flower shop and created unique arrangements, enjoyed fame and even a kind of horticultural notoriety among those who parodied and mocked her arrangements.

Spry explained herself, "If to use a kale leaf for its fine modeling, a bunch of grapes for its exotic bloom, a spherical leek flower for its decisive shape, a bare branch for its delicate strength, is to like strange materials, then I am guilty, but not guilty of liking them for any perverse reason."

Among her many admirers was Beverley Nichols, the British gardener, writer and wit. He talked about "doing a Constance Spry" which is to say "standing before a bed of hydrangeas, when summer has fled, and seeing beauty in their pallid parchment blossoms. It means suddenly stopping in a country lane and noting for the first time a scarlet cadenza of berries, and fitting it, in one's mind's eye, into a pewter vase against a white wall. It means bouts with brambles, flirtations with ferns and carnival with cabbages."

Constance Spry was born in 1886. She had varied careers in health, joined the civil service during World War I and was headmistress of a school teaching young teen-aged girls who worked in factories. It was not until the 1920s that she began arranging flowers, and 1929 before she opened her first shop in London. In 1938 a group of New York society women invited her to open an establishment on East 64th Street between Park and Madison Avenues.

In August of that year Charlotte Cox, as she was then, and who later became my friend Charlotte Thwing of Hawley, began an apprenticeship there. She had always been interested in flowers and after two years at Mt. Holyoke College, and a European summer she enrolled at Stockbridge, part of the Massachusetts Agricultural College and later the University of Massachusetts, to study floriculture.

Charlotte described Constance Spry as "ordinary, not at all aristocratic. She did not present an impressive appearance. She had everyday common sense. She never wore a hat, but always had gloves and high heels - and always seemed to be rushing."

Photographs of her at that time show her as a solid, tweedy matron, but "she had a tremendous imagination and nothing stopped her," Charlotte said.

Charlotte spent long days on the top floor of the shop building working with two other young women. "They trained us. Almost everything was wired with very thin wire. The wire was to give you control."

She used dried material, seedpods, and vegetables and fruits. "You always had to remember that you were creating Art."

Charlotte remembers that Spry used any kind of container, watering cans, tea pots, baby shoes, baskets. "But the flowers were the main thing. The vase was essentially hidden. For example she would use a flat white vase with white flowers and trailing branches. Her arrangements were very clever and interesting, never dull."

Constance Spry's arrangements showed up at society weddings and in the windows at Bergdorf's, the fashionable department store on Fifth Avenue. "I don't remember that we ever did a funeral, although back then funerals were the bread and butter of the florist business. Of course there were weddings. Constance Spry did the wedding flowers when the Duke of Windsor, who had abdicated as King of England, married Wallis Simpson."

Just before the shop opened Brenda Frazier, one of the most beautiful and famous debutantes of the time, had her coming out party. "The arrangements for Brenda's party were very important. It was my job to take big magnolia leaves, and strip them so that only the veins were left. Then they were gilded," Charlotte said.

After her apprenticeship in New York, Charlotte returned to Holyoke where her father was a well-known doctor. In March 1939, when she was just 25, she opened her own shop, The Flower Bowl.

"I had gotten a fantastic education by observing. I think education can be caught, not always taught. No other florist was like mine – and I intended to educate the town. For my first Christmas I did arrangements in blue and silver – but never again," she laughed.

The war ended Constance Spry's New York shop, and marriage in 1941 changed Charlotte's career as well.

The thing that did not really change was Charlotte's approach to life – an approach she shared with Constance Spry who said,

"I want to shout out - Do what you please, follow your own star. Be Oriental if you want to be and don't if you don't want to be. Just be natural and gay and lighthearted and pretty and simple and overflowing and general and baroque and bare and austere and stylized and wild and daring and conservative and learn and learn and learn."

A Spring Walk

"Lets go for a walk," I said to my husband one fresh spring Sunday.

He looked at me with suspicion. "Is this a walk where you make up a list of chores for me?"

"No, no," I assured him. "Let's just take a constitutional while the sun is shining."

We put on our coats, but he continued to look suspicious.

"Shall we walk around the garden first?" I suggested.

He agreed and didn't even grumble when I pointed out the rocks that I wanted moved. We mourned over the *Chamaecyparis* that the deer had eaten. The four foot tall *Chamaecyparis obtusa*, also known as Hinoki false cypress, was an extravagant purchase. It is a slow grower and I longed to have a substantial specimen so I could really admire the unusual fanlike evergreen sprays. Now nothing was left but a nibbled nub.

The deer also feasted on most of the buds on the rhododendrons next to the Cottage Ornee., and munched on some of the thorny roses. We cheered that the fence we put up around the raspberries last fall had held up pretty well. Not much to do there.

Little rhubarb buds were poking through fallen leaves. I said the area around the rhubarb bed really needed some work. He agreed.

We looked at the huge limb that had broken off the ancient apple tree at the edge of the lawn. "I guess I'll have to take the chain saw to clean that up properly," he said.

"Ummm. And don't forget the big branch that fell on top of the compost pile," I said starting to smile.

He smiled back. "I'm really glad we're just taking a constitutional and not working out a chore list."

We both laughed and set off down the road where no more chores were visible.

Acknowledgements

This is my first book, but over the years many people have taught, inspired and encouraged, bringing me to this point. I owe thanks to Denny Wilkins, my first editor at The Recorder whose red ink bled all over my first columns, as well as to editors like Rob Riggan who followed and my current editor Adam Orth who has supported the column in countless new ways.

Of course, I would not have gardens at all if it weren't for the gardeners who have come into my life like Helen Opie whose passion is organic vegetables, and Elsa Bakalar who introduced me to perennials. I owe thanks to countless others from neighbors who shared their plants, and Greenfield Garden Club members who laughed and groaned with me as they shared enthusiasms and knowledge.

I also thank those who have helped and advised me through the making of this book. B.J. Roche has been a neighbor, writing friend and adviser for years, known for tough love and encouragement. I owe special thanks to Carol Purington who was the first reader of each chapter and made each better and richer. I also thank Peter Beck, first among cheerleaders.

To paraphrase a song, if you become a mother by your children you'll be taught. I thank all five of my children, Philip, Chris, Diane, Betsy and Kate for enlarging my world and for teaching me perseverance. Chris gets an extra thank you for designing this book and handling the publishing technicalities.

Finally I thank my husband Henry for supporting my first tentative steps into the writing world, and every other adventurous step I have taken from the moment we met. I also thank him for the great drawings in the book. His sense of humor keeps us blooming in the garden – and everywhere else.

Complete Disclosure
Roses on the Rose Walk – Past and Present
*(in alphabetical order – the * indicates currently surviving)*

Abraham Darby – David Austin
* *Agnes* - Rugosa
* *Alba semi-plena* – Alba
* *Alchemyst* - Climber
Alexander Mackenzie – Canadian Explorer
* *Alli's Pink* - Farmgirl
Amiga Mia – Griffith Buck
* *Apart* – Rugosa
* *Applejack* – Griffith Buck

* *Belle Amour* - Damask
* *Belle Poitvine* – Rugosa
* *Blanc Double de Coubert* – Rugosa
* *Blaze* - Climber
* *Buckland Rose* - Farmgirl

Camaieux - Gallica
* *Cardinal Richelieu* - Gallica
* *Carefree Beauty* – Griffith Buck
* *Celestial* - Alba
* *Celsiana* - Damask
* *Champlain* – Canadian Explorer
Chapeau de Napoleon - Moss
* *Charlemont Rose* – Farmgirl
Charles de Mills - Gallica
Comtesse de Murinas - Moss
Constance Spry – David Austin
* *Corylus* – Rugosa

Darlow's Enigma - Climber
* *Dart's Dash* - Rugosa
* *De la Grifferai* - Rambler
Duchesse d'Angouleme - Gallica

Fair Bianca – David Austin
Felicite Parmentier - Alba
* *Fantin-Latour* - Alba
* *The Fairy* - Polyantha

* *Gentle Persuasion* – Griffith Buck
* *Ghislaine de Feligonde* – Multiflora rambler
* *Goldbusch* – Kordes
Graham Thomas – David Austin

* *Harrison's Yellow*
* *Hawkeye Belle* – Griffith Buck
Heritage – David Austin

* *Ispahan* - Damask

* *John Cabot* – Canadian Explorer

* *Knockout red*
* *Konegin von Danemark (Queen of Denmark)* - Alba

La Ville de Bruxelles - Damask
* *Leda* – Damask
Linda Campbell - Rugosa

* *Mabel* – Farmgirl
Madame Hardy – Damask
Madame Isaac Pereiere – Bourbon
* *Madame Legras de St. Germain* - Alba
* *Madame Plantier* - Alba
Madame Zoetmans - Damask
* *Mafalda Rose* – Farmgirl
Marie de Blois - Moss
* *Martin Frobisher* - Rugosa
* *Mary Rose* – David Austin
Maytime – Griffith Buck
* *Meidiland Scarlet* - Landscape
* *Meidiland White* - Landscape
* *Mrs. Doreen Pike* – David Austin
* *Mount Blanc* – Rugosa

* *New Dawn* - Climber
Nymphenburg – Kordes

Othello – David Austin

* *Passionate Nymph's Thigh* - Alba
* *Pink Grootendorst* – Rugosa
Perdita – David Austin
* *Prairie Harvest* – Griffith Buck
* *Purington Pink* – Farmgirl
* *Purington pink rambler* - Farmgirl

* *Queen Elizabeth* - Grandiflora

* *Rachel's Rose* – Farmgirl
* *Rachel's Other Rose* - Farmgirl
Robusta – Kordes
* *Rosa gallica officinalis* - Gallica
* *Rosa Glauca*
Rosa setigira - Climber
Rosa Mundi - Gallica
Roserie de l'Hay - Rugosa
Ruskin - Rugosa

Scabrosa - Rugosa
* *Sitka* – Rugosa
Sunny June - Shrub

* *Terri's Pink* - Farmgirl
* *Therese Bugnet* – Rugosa
Tuscany Superb - Gallica

Wife of Bath – David Austin
* *Wild Ginger* – Griffith Buck
* *William Baffin* – Canadian Explorer
* *Woodslawn Pink* – Farmgirl

This list is not constant from year to year. Roses come and go and as the winters are getting warmer I'm willing to try some roses again. I'm hoping this list might be useful to readers who want to plant their own hardy roses, keeping in mind that I live in Zone 5b where winter temperatures can fall to –15.

More Reading

Classic Roses: An illustrated encyclopedia and grower's manual of old roses, shrub roses and climbers

by Peter Beales. Holt, Rinehart and Winston, New York, 1985 432 pp.

The first sections of the book deal with the history and evolution of the rose, the ways roses have been used in the landscape, and how to grow and care for roses. The Dictionary section has useful illustrations of many cultivars of the various old rose varieties. Excellent index.

Climbing Roses

by Christopher Warner, Globe Pequot Press, Chester, Connecticut 1988 144 pages

Many good photographs of more climbing roses than I never knew existed. Basic advice about caring for climbers, as well as information about specific roses.

Climbing Roses

by Stephen Scanniello and Tania Bayard, Prentice Hall 1994 262 pages

Scanniello was the Brooklyn Botanic Gardens rosarian. The book gives information about care and uses of climbers, as well as information and photos of specific varieties.

The English Roses: Classic favorites and new selections

by David Austin Special photography by Howard Rice and Andrew Lawson Timber Press 2005 301 pp.

Gorgeous photos of the roses hybridized by David Austin, most of which are too tender to survive for long in Heath.

Glory of Roses

by Allen Lacy with Photographs by Christopher Baker, Stewart Tabori and Chang 1990 239 pp.

Gorgeous photographs with charming history of the rose, of rose growers and rose lovers, how roses are used in garden, and what they mean to us, and to those in the past.

continued

Hardy Roses: An Organic Guide to Growing Frost and Disease Resistant Varieties

By Robert Osborne with photography by Beth Powning Garden Way Publishing, 1991 138pp

Osborne has a nursery in New Brunswick, Canada and knows a lot about which hardy roses are good for the garden, from climbers to low shrubs. Beautiful photographs to help make choices. Full information about caring for roses including propagation.

Pink Ladies and Crimson Gents:
Portraits and Legends of 50 Roses

by Molly and Don Glentzer. Clarkson Potter Publishers 2007 144 pp.

Beautiful photographs and charming biographies of the gods and goddesses, literary, artistic and historic characters including noted gardeners who have given their names to roses from Ophelia and Omar Khayyam to Gertrude Jekyll and Graham Thomas.

The Old Rose Adventurer:
The Once Blooming Old European Roses and More

by Brent C. Dickerson. Timber Press 1999 616 pp.

After a brief introduction Dickerson launches into a fascinating and readable description and history of hundreds of individual roses. Useful appendices classify them by year of naming or entering into the written record, by breeder, or by color.

Otherwise Normal People:
Inside the thorny world of competitive rose gardening

By Aurelia C. Scott Algonquin Books of Chapel Hill 2007 235 pp.

Rose gardeners may be obsessive, but none are more so than those who compete for honor at rose shows. Informative and fun.

The Rose Bible

by Rayford Clayton Reddell with photographs by Robert Galyean Chronicle Books 1998 252 pp.

Another encyclopedic book with a history of roses, descriptions and photographs of great roses, antique, modern, ramblers, and Reddell own list of Fifty Immortal Roses. The final section describes, planting, maintenance and propagation.

A Rose by Any Name:
The little-known lore and deep-rooted history of rose names

by Douglas Brenner & Stephen Scanniello Algonquin Books 2009 320 pp.

In addition to history there is romance, hoax and scandal in this charming book which will reveal the personalities behind those as well known as Fantin-Latour as those as little known as Madame Ferdinand Jamin.

Roses: A Celebration

edited by Wayne Winterrowd with illustrations by Pamela Stagg North Point Press 2003 259 pp.

Delightful essays by 33 writers on their favorite rose, or Christopher Lloyd's explanation of why he removed the rose garden from his famous Great Dixter estate.

Smith & Hawken: 100 Old Roses for the American Garden

by Clair G. Martin with photographs by Saxon Holt. Workman Publishing 1999 277 pp.

Good history, description and photographs of 100 old roses. Information about growing roses, as well as fragrance and hardiness.

Rose Nurseries and Resources

The Antique Rose Emporium
P.O. Box 143
Brenham, TX 77833
www.antiqueroseemporium.com

Ashdown Roses Inc.
P.O. Box 129
Campobello, SC 29322
www.ashdownroses.com
email: roses@ashdownroses.com

Chamblee's Rose Nursery
10926 U.S. Hwy 69 North
Tyler, TX 75706
www.chambleeroses.com

Garden Valley Ranch
498 Pepper Road
Petaluma, CA 94954
www.gardenvalley.com

Hartwood Nursery
335 Hartwood Road
Fredericksburg, VA 22406
www.Hartwoodroses.com

Heirloom Roses
24062 NE Riverside Drive
St. Paul, OR 97137
www.heirloomroses.com

Heritage Rosarium
211 Haviland Mill Rd
Brookville MD 20833

High Country Roses
P.O. Box 148
Jensen, Utah 84035
www.highcountryroses.com
email: roses@easilink.com

Rogue Valley Roses
www.roguevalleyroses.com

Roserie at Byfields
PO Box R]
Waldoboro, ME 04572
Roses Unlimited
Laurens, South Carolina
www.rosesunlimitedownroot.com

Vintage Gardens
Antique and Extraordinary Roses
2833 Old Gravenstein Hwy.
South Sebastopol
California 95472
www.vintagegardens.com

RESOURCES

American Rose Society
www.ars.org

Canadian Rose Society
www.canadianrosesociety.org

World Federation of Rose Societies
www.worldrose.org

Griffith Buck Rose Website
http://www.ag.iastate.edu/centers/cad/rose1.html

HelpMeFind
www.helpmefind.com/roses

Roger's Roses Reference
www.rogersroses.com

The Heritage Rose Foundation
www.heritagerosefoundation.org

www.ingramcontent.com/pod-product-compliance
Lightning Source LLC
LaVergne TN
LVHW091203080426
835509LV00006B/811